Philosophising

Philosophising by Accident

Interviews with Élie During

Bernard Stiegler

Edited and Translated by Benoît Dillet

EDINBURGH
University Press

Edinburgh University Press is one of the leading university presses in the UK. We publish academic books and journals in our selected subject areas across the humanities and social sciences, combining cutting-edge scholarship with high editorial and production values to produce academic works of lasting importance. For more information visit our website: edinburghuniversitypress.com

Edinburgh University Press Ltd
The Tun – Holyrood Road, 12(2f) Jackson's Entry, Edinburgh EH8 8PJ

Typeset in 10.5/13pt Monotype Baskerville by
Servis Filmsetting Ltd, Stockport, Cheshire,
and printed and bound in Great Britain by
CPI Group (UK) Ltd, Croydon CR0 4YY

A CIP record for this book is available from the British Library

ISBN 978 1 4744 0822 6 (hardback)
ISBN 978 1 4744 0824 0 (webready PDF)
ISBN 978 1 4744 0823 3 (paperback)
ISBN 978 1 4744 0825 7 (epub)

Published with the support of the University of Edinburgh Scholarly Publishing Initiatives Fund.

Contents

Notes on the English Translation

The set of radio interviews that compose this book do not pose a lot of problems for the translator since Bernard Stiegler purposefully used a plain language to make his philosophical ideas available to a larger audience. However, I did have to simplify some sentences, or split them, to make them more fluent in English. Stiegler's language is quite logical as it moves by blocks; each concept or neologism refers to a specific philosopher or period in his thought, making it easy for the reader to witness the development of his thought.

I avoided adding too many endnotes to clarify specific points but I would like to draw the attention of readers to the translation of specific words or expressions that could help in understanding the text. Following Christopher Johnson, I have used 'externalisation' for *extériorisation* since 'external' is commonly used in English and not in French, and it also flows much better. I have translated *esprit* as 'spirit' but it should also be understood as 'mind' in the English sense, related to the intellect and cognition. For Stiegler, *esprit* is larger than the domain of the understanding (in Kantian terms), and his use of the term is a conscious move to reintroduce older questions, to relate his own work to other, older, traditions in philosophy. This move is aligned with that in Derrida's book on the concept of spirit/mind in Heidegger.[1] I have used 'medium' to translate the French word *support* which can be translated in English by a multitude of words depending on the context: support, prop, stand, aid (like visual aid but also teaching aid) and medium. Medium is more polyvalent than the other options, so I kept this, but the other meanings should be recalled when this term is used. I have translated *parole* as 'speech' and *paroles* sometimes as 'speech' or 'words'.

---

[1] Jacques Derrida, *Of Spirit: Heidegger and the Question*, trans. Geoffrey Bennington and Rachel Bowlby (Chicago: University of Chicago Press, 1991).

I draw attention to this since for structuralists (influenced by a certain reading of Saussure) the opposition between *langue* and *parole*, language and speech, was central; Stiegler is arguing after Derrida, however, that single language speech production (*parole*) is conditioned by and in continuity with the written word that corresponds to a system of signs (*langue*). I have translated *inconscience* as 'unawareness' or 'unconsciousness', but the polysemy present in the French word should also be kept in mind. Stiegler is using the word *inconscience* to refer to the psychoanalytic conception of the unconscious, but it also bears a normative edge when he denounces the thoughtlessness or reckless dimensions of science and other practices (especially in Chapter 4). He implicitly calls for a deeper understanding that takes into consideration the unconscious but it is also a call to take responsibility. 'Unawareness' is insufficient and perhaps even misleading since he explicitly rejects the Marxist conception of awareness. In this sense there is no awareness or consciousness that could save one from this condition of *inconscience*. I have also marked out words in English in the original with italics and with a star (*).

Finally, I would like to thank Bernard and Caroline Stiegler for their help and trust, Carol Macdonald for agreeing straight away to publish this translation with Edinburgh University Press, the two anonymous reviewers for their comments and corrections, Gerald Moore for the initial support, Anaïs Nony for her suggestions and the camaraderie, and Julia Elsky for her interest and for reading early drafts. Finally, *shukriya* Tara for helping me immensely throughout, especially in the final editing stages.

Translator's Introduction: Radiographing Philosophy

This series of interviews between Bernard Stiegler and Élie During was first broadcast in 2002 on France Culture, a renowned French public radio station that serves as a platform for academics and non-academics (cultural journalists) to discuss at length extremely diverse topics: from the most recent political news to the most esoteric and specialised topics. Élie During, who was writing a PhD dissertation on Bergson and Einstein at that time at the University of Paris 10 Ouest Nanterre, was fascinated with 'the speculative ambition of Stiegler and the breadth of his philosophical project' and felt in the position of a 'participant observer' during these interviews, to use the ethnographic expression.[1] The purpose of these interviews was to introduce to a wider audience the philosophical ideas and concepts worked out in the three volumes of the *Technics and Time* series. This book, first published in French in 2004, closed the first period of Stiegler's philosophy and together with *Passer à l'acte* (2003) and *Aimer, s'aimer, nous aimer* (2003) commenced a second period.[2] As Stiegler notes in the 2014 interview for this English edition, this second period worked at producing a new critique of political economy for the digital age. This new critique of political economy and his elements for an aesthetic theory developed in the *Symbolic Misery* series (2004–5) are directly derived from his fundamental thesis about tertiary retention (or third memory). While putting on hold the project of *Technics and Time*, he continued to draw from his working hypothesis and wrote his deconstruction of philosophy from the point of view of technics but in relation to contemporary political, economic and cultural events.

Radiographing Philosophy

'Philosophising by accident' is both the expression that best defines
Stiegler's own approach in philosophy and the philosophical practice on
radio in general. Undoubtedly, relations between philosophy and radio
have a long history in the twentieth century, both in France and in other
countries; depending on the traditions, philosophers have invested in or
resisted the pedagogical and political possibilities of the medium. The
intentions of radiographing philosophy differ from those of writing books
of philosophy. The transmission of philosophical debates and discourse
on the radio waves hopes to reach audiences beyond the lecture theatres
and the library lovers. Radio 'delocalizes philosophy from within'[3] by
seeking the accidental listener who will synchronise for a moment his or
her own time to the radio programme and the ideas at stake.

As the cultural theorist John Mowitt notes, radio was a problem
discussed widely in different philosophical traditions – in particular by
Martin Heidegger, Theodor Adorno, Walter Benjamin, Bertolt Brecht,
Georg Lukács and Jean-Paul Sartre.[4] While it was an object of philosophical reflection, the cultural studies of radio were quickly devalued in
the twentieth century, eclipsed by television and cinema studies.

In the case of philosophy in the French language, France Culture
has a singular role to play in instituting philosophy as a living discipline.
First created in 1963, France Culture as a radio station has produced
a parallel space or institution, and woven contiguous relations with the
virtual space of readers. There is a maieutic process at work between
the flow of philosophical radio programme and the flow of the listener's
consciousness. Listening is not passive but an active selection of elements
from the point of view of psycho-collective memories and expectations.
The listener is thus always potentially a reader as well as a speaker or a
writer of philosophy; he or she can act out this potential from the radio-
graphical impulse.

In evaluating the significance of this book by Stiegler in his larger
corpus, one needs to take into consideration the institutive and constitutive significance of France Culture for French philosophy as an
academic discipline and a form of thought. France Culture is defined as
a 'supply-based radio',[5] at least in its official mission statement. It does
not aim at running after ratings but at providing access to academic
disciplines and knowledge that are otherwise confined within the walls
of French Republican institutions (the Sorbonne, Collège de France,

EHESS and ENS amongst others). France Culture also differs from the pedagogical model of Radio-Sorbonne, created in 1947 as a proto-MOOC that broadcast in Paris university lectures from the Sorbonne.

The role of radio stations for philosophy in the French language is quite exceptional but absolutely ignored and understudied; it is as if the radio form were not as respectable as the book form for academic discourse. The history of philosophy on radio is much longer than that of blogs or online groups (such as on Facebook), and its audience is more diverse and accidental in constitution.

In an important study in French intellectual history, Tamara Chaplin examines the role of television for philosophy in France, where she turns to key philosophical moments that took place on television, and how French philosophers tried to repurpose television for pedagogical aims or for relaying their theses.[6] By providing a unique platform for authors and publishers to advertise their latest books, cultural shows broadcast on television and radio may partly be seen as marketing. Indeed, marketing became a central strategy particularly with the cultural show *Apostrophes*, created in 1975 and presented by Bernard Pivot (the last show was broadcast in June 1990). During one of its most memorable episodes, devoted to the work of new philosophers Bernard Henri-Lévy, André Glucksmann and Maurice Clavel, presenter Pivot held the books of his guests one by one in front of the camera and admitted, in response to Xavier Delcourt (co-author of *Contre la nouvelle philosophie*), that if showing books on television is advertising, then he is entirely for it. New philosophy was nothing other than the introduction of marketing in philosophy.[7] Yet the effects of France Culture on philosophical debates go far beyond the commerce of books, and the interviews with Stiegler contained in this book testify to this. Chaplin argues convincingly that televised philosophy should be considered as an integral part of the history of French thought, to avoid commonsensical arguments that flatten out differences, such as it is a French particularity to give philosophy a space on television and so on. These banal arguments fail to distinguish philosophical moments from the all-purpose intellectuals who talk endlessly on topics outside their area of expertise. Television and the radio feed on these all-purpose figures who have to comment on everything and give their positions on everything (and if the guests are male, the positioning seems even more convincing). On the contrary, to understand how philosophical discourse has metamorphosed in the twentieth and twenty-first centuries, it is productive to follow the movements of philosophy in different media.

The specific technological condition of philosophy in France has been essential in establishing debates and organising differential transmissions of philosophy. Stiegler's concepts provide some elements to account for the contiguous relations between philosophy and the media, especially as these analogical and digital technologies condition the transmission of knowledge. Stiegler's radio lectures compiled in this volume are anchored in a long-standing history of radio lectures or interviews given by famous French philosophers in the second half of the twentieth century: from Sartre's early radio shows on *La tribune des temps modernes* from October to December 1947 or Merleau-Ponty's *World of Perception* in October and November 1948, to the regular interviews with major French philosophers where Emmanuel Levinas, Marcel Gabriel, Jean-Toussaint Desanti, Vladimir Jankélévitch, Alexandre Koyré, Raymond Aron, Gaston Bachelard, Jean-François Lyotard and Louis Althusser presented their latest books.[8] It is extremely difficult to assess the reception or the significance of these interviews and radio appearances, but the radio created the conditions for philosophical dialogues (though overwhelmingly Parisian and male-centred) outside the usual academic organs (lectures, conferences, journals, books). However, the effect of radio on French thought should not be overemphasised and exaggerated: its role has remained minoritarian, and philosophy on radio is a marginal and exceptional phenomenon. Its official function is to provide strata of the general public with access to the words of these professors or philosophers; it attempts to integrate and reach out to territories that are poor in cultural and intellectual life. The possibility of listening, of tuning in, gives France Culture and philosophy radio programmes their pedagogical role. The relationship between those in the radio studio and the listeners differs radically from that of classrooms. The audience of the radio programmes is by definition unknown and not physically present or immediately recognisable, but the programmes and their cultivated relationship are not devoid of heuristic processes. Radio is particularly fit for philosophical practice as a self-training exercise, since 'philosophizing is first and foremost an autodidactic activity'.[9] The intended audience differs from traditional monographic publications: it is not necessarily more democratic or diverse but accidental in constitution, probably more so before the invention of podcasts and the creation of vast archives in the early 2000s (where radio shows can be listened to sometimes years afterwards).[10]

The very practice of 'radiographing philosophy' in these interviews with During is doubled by a philosophising of radio. The cadence and the tonality of Stiegler's words are already conditioned by the technical infrastructure of social and individual life, what Simondon called the 'associated milieu'. More importantly, by radiographing Stiegler's arguments and words, these interviews serve as an introduction or as a road map to his other, longer, works. Instead of being an abbreviated or washed out version of the arguments from the substantive *Technics and Time* series, the orality of the medium gives a particular rhythm, tone and effervescence to these interviews. While Stiegler repeats his arguments throughout his books, each time he adds one more element to continue to develop his project of deconstructing metaphysics from the point of view of technics – it is the repetition of difference and not repetition of the same.[11] It is with this technical apparatus that philosophy can take a new dimension and participate in everyday life beyond the book form; it is a different way of writing and circulating philosophical discourse.

Radiographing philosophy means that philosophers supplement their discourse and open it to the work of translators and mediators, not to adapt the philosophical discourse to the radio temporality but to adopt the technical apparatus, with all its incompressible constraints, to create accidentally and incidentally new circuits of individuation. A radio of philosophy always already works at a philosophy of radio, where the border between one sphere and the other withers away. It is not that by going in the radio studios philosophers have finally accepted to be more concrete and in the real world, as if philosophy was opposed to reality, as its big Other. This is an illusion to conceive the possibility of a knowledge independent from reality itself. Reality does not exist outside philosophy and philosophy is written in the present; even new readings of old texts attempt to reactivate something for the present condition.[12] Radiographing philosophy is therefore not disseminating philosophical reflections packaged especially for the radio format, with all its editorial and technical constraints, but it is a continuation of philosophy by other means. It is one more way to philosophise for different purposes and with different expectations. As mentioned earlier, the movement of philosophical thought in France today is partly constituted by this radio space. It is a space that is not reducible to academic discourse – to the domain of academic journals, conferences, books, letters and other practices – but that is not accessible to all either, at least *de facto*. Stiegler refers to the listeners of France Culture as a privileged few, those that are proletarianised but who are trying to fight it, or at least think that they are working in this direction.[13]

An entire social life of concepts takes place on radio, participating in the constitution of philosophy as a situation of object, places and practices. As the French sociologist Jean-Louis Fabiani rightly argues, 'major philosophers only exist through the minor ones, who are both an audience and a double, that is, well-founded social anchors'.[14]

It is a different kind of writing, a writing without hands[15] or an augmented gesture, that is paced according to the recording device. Until the invention of tape recorders and podcasts, radio was a continuous flux with no possibility for the listener to return to the previous sentence or the previous paragraph. The linearity of radio brought new cadences into philosophy as a living practice, especially after the Second World War. Radio also changed quite fundamentally with the arrival of television, and then with computers and the internet; it had to find a new place in this new reticularity. While readings and live drama performances were much more common before television and the internet, those formats became quickly outdated as the demand for more interactive and original content grew. We find traces, both digital and analogue, of the platform that France Culture was, has been and, to a large extent, continues to be. While a few studies have been published on France Culture as a public service, as an institution, and the evolution of its radio programmes, none of them have really accounted for its influence on 'French' philosophy.[16] A whole history of radio philosophy in France remains to be done. It is another space for philosophy to live and prosper, relaying one philosopher after another, one theme after another, in the movement of a desire that cannot be fully relayed. The listeners' expectations (or their psycho-collective protentions) are produced and shaped in different ways from the community of readers, or maybe they become readers after being listeners, or they become intermittently both readers and listeners.

Radiographing philosophy means to create the possibility for the eruption of the inessential, the extra or the supplement in the everyday. The question interrupts the banal gestures and activities of the everyday. The contact on the radio with philosophy is not immediate and given, but it is cultivated with the help of its intercessors. Turning on the radio to find the exceptionality and the accidentality of thought – in fact we always turn on the radio by accident (even when it is programmed by the alarm clock) – the programmes converge into a seamless stream.

The role of France Culture has metamorphosed over the decades: some regret the good old times and the decline in quality, others find it elitist and out of touch with current realities.[17] No doubt listeners have divergent opinions about the ethos of the radio station, but many amateurs engage with specific shows during their free time, they write about them on blogs and (more recently) in the comment sections on the France Culture website, they upload them on YouTube or Soundcloud, others transcribe whole discussions from radio shows on amateur websites, and even mailing-lists of listeners were formed.[18] When the detractors call France Culture elitist, patronising, paternalist, idealist or, worse, archaic, it is assumed that other forms of short-circuiting of thought are deemed more realistic and 'modern'. But on the contrary, by being 'supply-based' it intends to avoid the logic of the market without falling into its other extreme, complete independence and autonomy, since it intends to remain on air and open to everyone in an accessible language and format. For instance, Adèle Van Reeth, who has led the daily philosophy programme *Les Nouveaux chemins de la connaissance* ('The New Paths of Knowledge'), explains this objective:

I have such a curiosity towards what I want to discover, learn, transmit, and I work so much in choosing the right possible means to communicate [*faire entendre*] this thought that I want to give a voice, that there is not much room for deception. Had a programme lacked some technical rigour? Maybe, but then we would have reached the audience who is put off by the jargon. Another programme, on the contrary, turns out to be too dry, technical and exclusive for those who do not know the topic? Then perhaps I would have brought something to the most advanced [*aguerris*] listeners, and I would have reminded the others that philosophy is both an eloquent and a demanding exercise. . . . My only goal: to make thought as lively as possible.[19]

Stiegler envisages radio as a technical milieu with the capacity to transmit knowledge, experience or spirit in general. This technical milieu is the condition and the support for individual and collective memories. It is a *hypomnesis* that allows for *anamnesis*, following his understanding of the relation between *hypomnesis* and *anamnesis*: '*anamnesis* is the good way of practising *hypomnesis*'.[20] Though derived from the same root (*mneme* in Greek means 'memory'), *hypomnesis* and *anamnesis* are often opposed in the history of philosophy. In simple terms, *hypomnesis* is dead memory carried by diverse material supports (also called *hypomnemata*) and *anamnesis*, or reminiscence, is living memory. These two concepts are crucial for Stiegler in his dialogue with Plato's discourse on writing as well as with Derrida, and his work can be read as a long-standing explication of Derrida (his doctoral supervisor) but also Gérard Granel. Philosophers forget about *hypomnesis* in arguing for a purer and more noble technique of thought, *anamnesis*. This opposition, which Derrida started to deconstruct in *Of Grammatology* and 'Plato's Pharmacy', runs as an Ariadne's thread in philosophy: philosophers have repressed the question of technics (or *hypomnesis*) in philosophical discourse (as *anamnesis*).[21] This repression or forgetting of technics and technical objects is extremely problematic for Stiegler since humans have no qualities and no interiority but find a sense of purpose through their external relations with tools and *hypomnemata*. Technical objects are everywhere, making up an associated milieu that humans can only escape intermittently. This supplemented milieu can also become dissociated when the technical individuation dissociates itself from the individual and collective individuation, necessitating a readjustment between the technical and the cultural systems. Even before computers and the internet, any given writer has always been surrounded with *biblia*, material supports of spirit that open it to other memories, minds and thoughts that preceded her/him. Stiegler is deeply interested in *biblia* as material objects but also in all the techniques that writers have developed to materially annotate, correlate, classify and organise their thoughts and their fallibility. He called this organisation of space that took place *before* the writing and the publication of books 'a retentional and virtual space'.[22] Immersed in this retentional and virtual space, the writer can therefore convert in all improbability his or her lack into necessities by producing singularities and add to the diversity of ideas (or consistences). But writers are only one example of uses of *hypomnemata*; Stiegler explains that technics has always had a central role for humans as a palliative for the lack of human origin, which can never be filled.[23]

He often refers to this in relation to his interpretation of the myth of Prometheus and Epimetheus:

This accidental forgetting, generator of prostheses and artifices making up for a lack of origin, is equally the origin of hypomnesis, to which Plato will later oppose the anamnesis of the origin.[24]

In the myth, it is precisely because Epimetheus forgets to give humans qualities that Prometheus steals fire (hence technics) from Zeus to palliate for this lack of qualities. This accidental forgetting is overcome by an accidental production of prostheses and artifices. Following Derrida, Stiegler argues that writing and *hypomnemata* in general, although in different ways, are *pharmaka*, both a poison and a cure. He reminds us that late in his life and work, from *The Republic* onwards, Plato left the tragic culture by trying to eliminate the pharmacological aspects of writing as well as all technics in general (music and poetic arts) by submitting them to the power of dialectics.[25] This is partly why radio is a well-suited technical milieu for Stiegler to outline some of his main theses and hypotheses about technical objects and memory, the origin of philosophy, the synchronisation of consciousnesses and the technoscientific unconscious of contemporary science. By 'philosophising by accident', Stiegler means that accidentality was decisive in his own 'becoming-philosopher' – as he called it[26] – but beyond the self-centric narration of his trajectory in philosophy, he attempted to define philosophy *in general* as always beginning with the accident. Accidentality is not only astonishment, or even the disposition or passion that started all philosophising for Aristotle. It is perhaps Stiegler's astonishment at converting a working hypothesis into a thesis, into a fully fleshed out position in the philosophical domain,[27] that led him to repeat his arguments book after book in order to find the originary impulse that led him to philosophise. This is a hypothesis since it is fallible and im-probable. Stiegler's thought is a philosophy of fallibility, what he calls 'the necessary default' (*le défaut qu'il faut*). This surprise has not left him, and his desire to share this original accidental impulse is not to self-proclaim his status as philosopher but, by publicly remembering it, to find again in himself and his traces, in his thought and his memory, as an *anamnesis*, to recover the path by which he arrived at the practice of philosophising. *This thesis is itself a pros-thesis*, a new transductive support constituted for a critical reader that comes after, since philosophising always takes place too late, as an after-thought after the accident. This retroaction is what psychoanalysts call *deferred action* or *afterwardness* (*Nachträglichkeit* in German or *après-coup* in French).[28] Stiegler emphasised the accidentality of his 'becoming-philosopher', but this accidentality is also at work in the radiographing of philosophy, when one tunes in by accident to discussions and dialogues inviting a philosophising.

To sum up the first part of this introduction: the radiographic dispositif in philosophy can be used in a positive manner to reach out to territories and lives that struggle against today's proletarianising tendencies. Large territories have been turned into deserts, where thoughts cannot grow.

In these interviews, Stiegler participates in a certain project of France Culture, which is of course not a singular project, but a platform composed of a multiplicity of projects that are often contradictory, to give consistency to philosophy through its programmes on philosophy. He joins the journalist-academics who, even in other cultural programmes that are not strictly devoted to philosophy but where philosophers are often referred to and have a ghostly presence, resist the present state of affairs.

The Birth of a Philosophy

For Stiegler, the question remains 'what is philosophy?' since *Philosophising by Accident* is first and foremost an introduction to his conception of philosophy. He begins to philosophise outside certain French Republican institutions that participate in the atrophying of thought, and that, in the name of tradition and classicism, vacuum away the rest of society. Everyone can philosophise – there is no strict prerequisite, to have studied at Oxford, Cambridge or École Normale Supérieure – yet many have an interest in keeping philosophy out of reach of the masses. This elitism and classicism is fought by Stiegler in his very bastardisation of philosophy: accessing by accident a domain which he should never have been invited to. It is through developing a technique of reading (Ian James calls it 'technique of thought'[29]) that he re-appropriated philosophy so as to open it to the technical conditioning of life. I will analyse here how his entire philosophical thought is based on developing a technique of reading that will allow him to approach difficult texts and thoughts (Mallarmé, Husserl, Heidegger, Derrida). There is a technicity and a desire to gather thoughts and compile elements of other spirits. I use 'spirit' here deliberately since Stiegler attempts to reactivate, after Derrida, this outdated notion that was surpassed by 'mind' or other rational lexicon. Stiegler's entire thought is technical or prosthetic, using different concepts to reconsider the transductive relations between technics and thought.[30] In every respect, it is dealing with the complexity of technics and what it does to thought: *it unthinks thought*, every technical and technological shock overshadows thinking, reconfigures the operating field of thought. There is no inside or outside of philosophy but a co-constitutive enterprise of thinking and living: the large corporations and engineers making and designing technical objects capitalise on twenty-five centuries of philosophy. The project of *Technics and Time* begins in the trauma of the divide between *technē* and *epistēmē*, between practical knowledge such as craftsmanship or art on the one hand, and science or knowledge in general on the other. According to Stiegler, this divide began with metaphysics and Plato, and we can call this the first epistemological break of philosophy, insofar as Plato and Aristotle attempted to found philosophy as a science (*epistēmē*) purified from its non-dialectical and tragic origins in pre-Socratic thought. This led to a division of labour between intellectual work and manual work, reinforcing oppositions and dualisms in individual and collective bodies.

Like many other philosophers, for Stiegler, philosophy is both a psychic and a collective process of *anamnesis* to the extent that one reads oneself to remember who one was at the time of writing but also to produce new singularities or diachronies in the repetition of difference. After discussing Plato, Leroi-Gourhan and Husserl, developing his hypothesis about third memory or tertiary retention, and the technical constitution of the *already-there* and a past not lived but co-existing with the living in the first two interviews, Stiegler explains at length in Chapter 4 the notions of synchrony and diachrony that he develops in the second phase of his work after *Philosophising by Accident* – these notions are also called synchronisation and diachronisation since he understands these as tendencies rather than opposites. Synchrony is a necessary terrain for the cultivation of diachronies and to keep a tension between those two tendencies. These are rooted in post-Saussurian structuralism as well as Simondonian philosophy, and particularly the concepts of stability, instability and metastability.

Yet the relation between *anamnesis* and *hypomnesis* as discussed above is perhaps what distinguishes him from other philosophers. Stiegler's main task is to deconstruct philosophy and show how philosophers and philosophy repress technics, and to argue his hypothesis that humans are transductively made by technics. He calls this practice '[his] philosophy'.[31] This main project, a prosthetic deconstruction of philosophy, is always in the background, even in his recent and more politicised works. His conception and execution of critique is quite specific: he draws from moments of philosophy to find concepts and tools to think the present condition but always ends on the technological blindspots of these great thinkers, what they cannot and could not think.

This has huge consequences for Stiegler's own approach to philosophy in terms of periodisation and historicisation. By periodising the thought of specific thinkers, he seeks punctual interests and problems that are *epokhal de jure*, since they become suspended in the very corpus under study, in Plato, Marx, Freud, Heidegger and others, but that can return to the present, as an improbable haunting trace. This is constantly acknowledged and emphasised in his writings, a strong phenomenology of reading that drives his entire method and project, a reading that is always already a writing waiting to be read and written in the future. Once again, this is why the notion of *après-coup* or deferred action is central, given the bi-directionality of philosophy, retrogressive and progressive, the retentionality of the original letter that carries potentialities (or protentions) beyond itself and towards the future. It is tertiary retention (the technical support of memory) that provides 'the possibility of resuming an interrupted piece of work: which, for the phenomenologist, is always the work of the time of "filling-in" on the part of an intention intending an *eidos*'.[32] It provides the possibility to begin again one's work (of a past self) or the work of a previous philosopher with a fresh perspective. For example, in the third volume of *Technics and Time*, he executes a close reading of the 'Transcendental Deduction' section and in particular the triple synthesis in Kant's *Critique of Pure Reason* (apprehension, reproduction and recognition) and shows how they are conditioned by schematism. Kant does not see, according to Stiegler, the transformation of his own thinking in the first *Critique* between the first and the second editions (respectively 1781 and 1787) and how his own *hypomnemata* and idiotexts have altered the order of the synthesis itself, changing the course of his argument and obscuring the question of *hypomnesis* or technics.[33]

Stiegler's practice of critique inherits from the philosophers he reads, and particularly from structuralism and poststructuralism, but at their limits. In other words, he attempts to reactivate their thoughts not by simply repeating the same arguments but by exposing their limits and thinking at their limits. I called his philosophy prosthetic since he writes on to the philosophies that he reads, but the opposite is also true: he keeps in his language the concepts of other philosophers that he read and analysed in detail in other works. These close readings left marks on his own language (or idiolect). By trying to keep all these concepts, his writing sometimes makes for tortuous sentences – and many of his late works are also transcribed from oral dictation using a piece of software. His work bears the mark of this accumulation of readings and neologisms, making it difficult for the reader to approach his later and more recent work without understanding epiphylogenesis, tertiary retention, pharmacology, general organology, transindividuation, grammatisation, discretisation, quasi-cause, synchrony-diachrony, proletarianisation, the play of subsistence-existence-consistence, composition versus opposition, *hypomnesis* and idiotext.[34] All these concepts are introduced in these interviews in relation to their contexts and how they are used to dialogue with other philosophical traditions. In a sense, Stiegler is cannibalising other philosophies, reintegrating them as his own, carrying their traces in his own prose, welding them into new prosthetic forms, for new purposes. To remain faithful to philosophy is to participate in it and to show its relevance, how its tools (the concepts) can be reworked and reactivated for particular struggles in the present. The archive of philosophy should therefore not be seen as inert, as simply a *hypomnesis*, but it can be individuated, through processes of psychic and collective *anamnesis*, a remembering or recollection that is always dia-logical:

One cannot be faithful to the unity and the identity of what remains constant throughout the alterities of the diverse characters one will have been and played, sometimes without knowing it, without noticing it, and which results from the accidental character of existence.[35]

Stiegler sometimes calls this '*différant* identification', to reflect this process of differed identification that is mobilised. Two concepts that he has not yet developed but always announces in passing are those of context and idiotext. He explains in different places that the idiotext is imagined and speculated in the last volume of *Technics and Time* as a memory-flux since it appears as a spiral, a whirl-like figure prosthetically supported. His books are conceived as a single dorsal space which one can navigate, where every book is an introduction to a last volume to come, but which never comes. These series of interviews from 2002 are no exception, and commentaries on the virtual subsequent volumes of *Technics and Time*, aborted since 2001, haunt the dialogue between Stiegler and During. Serge Trottein is not entirely wrong when he refers to Stiegler's work as a collection of introductions and suspense, building up to the publication of *The Necessary Defaut* (*Le Défaut qu'il faut*) that continues to be delayed and may never be known.[36]

To give other examples of his critiques of philosophers: while Heidegger opened many avenues in thinking technics, Stiegler also critiques his denigration of technics to preserve 'traditional language' in his late texts.[37] More recently, in *States of Shock*, in a posthumous dialogue and homage to his friend Lyotard, Stiegler continues this prosthetic deconstruction by showing how the essay '*Logos* and *Techne*, or Telegraphy' (delivered in one of Stiegler's seminars in 1986 at Collège international de philosophie) opposes in a classical manner *anamnesis* and *hypomnesis* when it comes to new technologies (that Lyotard calls telegraphy – related to the technologies of reading that Stiegler was beginning to conceive during exhibitions at the Centre Georges Pompidou and then at INA).[38] Based on this reading of this text, Stiegler goes so far as to compare Lyotard's position to Heidegger's nostalgia for authenticity and cultural heritage. While perhaps opposing art and modern technology too starkly, Lyotard however ends at a position remarkably close to Stiegler's in a lesser-known lecture given at the Sorbonne in October 1985 where he discussed what new technologies do to art, especially in transforming the audience and the *We*.[39]

Stiegler's thought is more commonly discussed in dialogue with Derrida's work, especially on the question of his reading and borrowing of Derrida's concepts. By drawing extensively on Derrida's *Of Grammatology*, he repeatedly argued that he felt more faithful than Derrida himself to the very project of grammatology. This already appears in an important moment in the second volume of *Technics and Time* when he questions the role of the originary trace – that was there all along. It is on this aspect that Stiegler begins to conceive of his work as a crucial bifurcation from or excrescence on Derrida's thought, with the grafted notion of grammatisation (from Sylvain Auroux). For Derrida, grammatisation is what the project of grammatology should have been, the history of supplements rather than the interpellation of arche-writing or arche-trace. Here is an early interrogation worth quoting at length:

Grammatology lays out a logic of the supplement in which supplementary accidentality is originary. The history of the supplement must be understood as awkward, accidental history whose result would be an essential-becoming of the accident – but which would also require speaking of an accidental-becoming of essence. But is the grammatological project not weakened in advance in frequently blurring phonological writing's specificity, in suggesting that most of the time virtually everything that takes place in it was always there beforehand, and in not making this specificity a central issue (and does all of grammatology not, in a certain sense, necessarily banish just such a question)? Does this not bring up the possible objection that in the end, the supplement will really not have been?[40]

The originary trace to all traces, or arche-trace, prevents the grammatological project from being a history of supplements and their occurrences. This also leads to fundamental disagreements on the status of history in philosophy, leading many scholars to debate Derrida's and Stiegler's positions vis-à-vis *différance*, temporality, the nonliving and the nonhuman. The debate on Derrida and Stiegler is crucial and gravitates around questions of empiricity and transcendentality (leading Stiegler to imagine an atranscendental philosophy).[41] It also led to disagreements about whether Stiegler is guilty of anthropocentrism and giving priority to humans over animals in their relations to tools and their technical constitution. Geoffrey Bennington, Tracy Colony and Nathan Van Camp argue that Derrida's concepts of *gramme*, *différance* and trace allow us to think beyond the animal-human opposition, while Stiegler reaffirms the exceptionality of the human.[42] These authors, however, fail to take into account his processual approach to the 'human'; he would even avoid the term ('human') due to the association with humanism, preferring the confusing double negation the 'non-inhuman' to refer to actions rather than to an essence or ontology. What interests Stiegler is less the human than the noetic processes of life. Far from being 'posthuman' or 'posthumanist', his philosophy attempts to leave these debates behind to focus on tendencies and processes of life, distinguishing for instance between entropic and negentropic orientations.

These are but a few examples of a long list of *readings* contained in his books. His later thought, especially since the third volume of *Technics and Time*, has sometimes been read as being catastrophic, pessimistic or alarmist. Stiegler turned to political economy with the *Disbelief and Discredit* series (2004–6) and more importantly with *For a New Critique of Political Economy* (2009), to aesthetics with the *Symbolic Misery* series (2004–5), to politics more openly with the *Constituer l'Europe* series (2005), *Télécratie contre démocratie* (2006), *De la démocratie participative* (2007) and *Pharmacologie du Front national* (2013), and finally to the question of the youth and educational systems with *Taking Care* (2008) and *L'École, le numérique et la société qui vient* (2012). Élie During anticipated Stiegler's political turn in his work when he asked a question about synchronisation of consciousnesses in a decisive moment of *Philosophising by Accident*, in the first question of the fourth interview (but also in the 2001 interview in the appendix). During voiced his disagreement about the uniformisation of behaviour and the theme of alienation 'even when it is dressed in a phenomenological register'.[43] Others, like Rancière in 2008, would distance themselves from Stiegler's supposedly classical Marxist (and therefore resentful) position that no longer suits the present. Rancière writes in an extremely provocative sentence that these resentful critical theorists portray 'the image, totally hackneyed and yet endlessly service-able, of the poor cretin of an individual consumer, drowned by the flood of commodities and images and seduced by their false promises'.[44] If this is partly aimed at Stiegler, and there are good reasons to think so, in this polemical but important chapter, Rancière entirely misinterprets Stiegler's diagnosis of the technical constitution and conditioning of critical thought (and also denies in other works the consequences and the significance of the technical reproducibility of art on aesthetic and art production). For Stiegler, however, the constitution and conditioning of technics is understood in a transductive way, and not simply in a uni-lateral and deafening way. Contrary to Richard Beardsworth's reading of Stiegler's politics, his position cannot be reduced to technological determinism.[45]

At one point, in the third volume of *Technics and Time* and relevant for us here, Stiegler is cautious to warn against demonising the US culture industry for the destruction of European consciousness. In his study of television and cinema, he emphasises the US domination in order to appreciate the inventive technological dispositif that this industry has created and that Europeans accept too passively.

Delegation of the operations of understanding to machines has taken place essentially under the influence of American industry. Yet we see nowhere in the current industrial brutality any consequences of this fact of a sudden alteration of consciousness, and even less a monstrous event. But consciousness is altera-tion. This does not mean that alteration might not lead to a monstrous state of things in turn leading toward the annihilation of this consciousness; we cannot exclude such a possibility – quite to the contrary. On the other hand, this pos-sibility of destruction is already contained in, is already a part of, consciousness itself: consciousness is this possibility, as a cinematic flux projecting its phantoms onto many screens.[46]

Stiegler's political thought is related to accidents and the potential for societies and civilisation to collapse. Emergencies also create the neces-sity for philosophising; Socrates began to philosophise after the defeat of Athens in the Peloponnesian War, and it is this deferred action or afterwardness that I referred to earlier. 'Philosophising by accident' is therefore the expression that sums up Stiegler's personal philosophi-cal experience as well as a call to take into consideration the accidents in noeticity, against hyper-rationalist projects that do not make room for the improbable, the inessential and the fallible. The facticity of the accident requires the development of techniques to convert it into a necessity, following Deleuze and Bosquet, as he explains once again in the interview from 2014 included as an appendix. Stiegler has good reasons to associate accidentality and facticity based on the philosophical anthropology of technical life presented in *Technics and Time, Vol. 1: The Fault of Epimetheus*. While humans and life are not born philosophising or making tools, they have the disposition or the potential to do so. This becoming-philosopher is in fact never fully realised but always in the making and processual. His work begins against the generally accepted idea that philosophy requires a professionalisation, first a classical training and then a career deemed successful by peers and the accepted norms: thinking always takes place with accidentality. Socrates' accident, that is, the Athenian decision to condemn him to death, had huge consequences for the history of philosophising.

Jean-François Lyotard in some introductory courses on philosophy given at the Sorbonne in 1964–5 displaces the usual question 'what is philosophy?' on to the more challenging one 'why philosophise?'. This new question also suits Stiegler's project that starts with knowledge as desire, or desire as knowledge (and both go back to Plato's *Symposium* and the relation between Alcibiades and Socrates).[47] In giving a social role to philosophy Lyotard warns his students against a retreat from the world and its transformations since there can be no escape from communication, exchange and desire.[48] Philosophising for Lyotard is to respond to the movement of desire that always resists and escapes theories of consciousness, mind or reason. It starts in the refusal of unity and purpose; questions about the purpose of philosophy always aim at killing desire and reinforcing the powers that be.

When Stiegler asks the question 'what is philosophy?', he presents at least two answers. First, in his work, philosophy is closely associated with the practice of teaching, since to philosophise is to individuate philosophy itself, to contribute by adding one more element: this can be done through the creation of concepts or neologisms, and by reactivating classical concepts to respond more directly to the present state of affairs. Stiegler has a singular understanding of the beginning of philosophy and metaphysics. He considers Plato the first one to have broken away from pre-Socratic thought and tragic culture by creating dialectics and inventing metaphysics (in Derrida's sense of the term). Hence when Stiegler discusses Plato's *Lesser Hippias*, regarded by specialists as Plato's first written work, he reads it as the first philosophy book. Commenting on the opening of *Lesser Hippias*, Stiegler writes: 'The first question philosophy asks . . . is not the question of being, [nor] is it that of becoming, nor technics . . . [it] is not about the law nor power, nor certainly about poetry. The first question that is not the first question (being generally made secondary) regards *teaching*.'[49] Philosophy is closely tied to the collective practice of teaching that leads both teachers and students to axioms and aporias, which are not accessible to rational or dogmatic approaches. It cannot be reduced to an autonomous discipline of expertise and tight-knit research communities. As the experience of the aporia, the impasse or the cul-de-sac, philosophical teaching is however neither straightforward nor guided by a *telos*, it is closer to an experiment and a way of life.[50] In this sense, the teacher and the student cultivate desire and a libidinal economy.

Second, philosophy is born according to him with Socrates, who developed his famous maieutic method of asking questions, and more specifically the question *ti esti?*, 'what is . . .?'.[51] France Culture can therefore be called the 'radio of questions', a good place for interviews and exchanges, triggering the very desire to ask questions. The value of philosophy decreased with the end of modernity and the transformation of institutions; the role of philosophy (questioning) is untimely since in the time of capital, the possibility of questioning is captured. The fact that the Google search engine is often a point of access for questions shows the conditioning and the discretion of philosophy. Google could not have existed without philosophy, mathematics and other disciplines. The practice of questioning (philosophy) has been inscribed and captured by the algorithms of the search engine itself. Think for instance about our collective stupor at the predictive function of this search engine, as if it revealed a secret, a collective unconscious. By typing in the search bar, we could have access to this immense collective raw data processed by Google's phenomenal algorithmic power and therefore find in this automated writing something meaningful about society, and the thoughts as well as the desires of our fellow comrades who use the very same tool in their everyday life. The indeterminacy of the future is captured, our dreams are 'cancelled' – as one of Banksy's murals in Boston, Massachusetts, reads. What the 1980s Punk movement called 'no future' should be understood less as a motto than as a symptom of the time. To philosophise today for Stiegler means to confront the fact that new generations hold 'no future' as their motto.[52] No future is the symptom

of a post-revolutionary generation that knows that their future will be
worse than their parents' but any attempt to envisage utopian projects or
the good life is deemed idealist, naive, patronising or, worse, totalitarian.
The impossibility of questioning constitutes philosophy's milieu, where
thinking begins in the realisation of this suffocation.[53] Such are the conditions of possibility and impossibility of philosophy for Stiegler, and the
very practice of philosophy amounts to an endless hermeneutic process
that interprets philosophers to the letter, not to repeat them and find the
exactitude of their thought but to interpret their words or concepts in
their spirit. The regime of law in philosophy is not made of contracts and
laws that are set once and for all (even when they are written in stone) but
it is a jurisprudence.[54] Philosophy is akin to a conceptual jurisprudence;
each concept is an ensemble of traces recording particular moods and
living conditions, both healthy and sick ones. In this hermeneutic and
jurisprudential conception of philosophy, accidents are omnipresent,
creating wounds (and 'traumatypes') waiting to be cured, even if provi-
sionally. Yet the regime of law in society, and possibly also in philosophy,
is not Kantian but Kafkian, as Laurent de Sutter notes:[55] in societies of
control, sources and causes of the regime of law are largely diffused and
disoriented, and the tools invoked (human rights, security) are reduced
to palliating symptoms and anxieties. This situation, partly driven by the
constant drive for automatisation, brings jurisprudence into crisis.

Accidentality was also central to Deleuze. In an unusual historicist
move, Deleuze refers to modern art as signalling the shift from essence
to accidents, something that for him is echoed more largely in thought,
and particularly in philosophy: 'Modern painting begins when man no
longer experiences himself as an essence, but as an accident.'[56] The rise
of specific intellectuals and the explosion of academic disciplines into
micro-topics and hyperspecialisms also redistributes the conditionality
of philosophy today. Although Stiegler generalises the accidental facticity of thought and philosophy, the degree and intensity of this accidentality has changed with the multiplication of technological shocks, and
the task of philosophy today is to talk about the accident and not the
essence.

Our fundamental relation to history has changed, much like the
place of philosophy as a social discipline, as a knowledge and a practice anchored in society. The title of the chapter from which Deleuze's
quotation was extracted reads powerfully: 'every painter recapitulates
the history of painting in his or her own way . . .'. Deleuze would have

certainly agreed that this statement can be extended to philosophy itself, that every philosopher indeed recapitulates the history of philosophy. Reading philosophers is to read them read other philosophers.

Notes

1. Personal communication with Élie During, 5 June 2015.
2. These two short books published respectively in June and October 2003 were translated and compiled in Bernard Stiegler, *Acting Out*, trans. David Barison, Daniel Ross and Patrick Crogan (Stanford: Stanford University Press, 2008).
3. John Mowitt, *Radio: Essays in Bad Reception* (Berkeley: University of California Press, 2011), p. 76.
4. Mowitt, *Radio*.
5. Philippe Meyer, 'Il faut stopper la dérive à Radio France', *Le Monde*, 27 March 2015.
6. Tamara Chaplin, *Turning On the Mind: French Philosophers on Television* (Chicago: University of Chicago Press, 2007).
7. '[The new philosophers] do have a certain newness about them: rather than form a school, they have introduced France to literary and philosophical marketing.' Gilles Deleuze, 'On the New Philosophers (Plus a More General Problem)', in *Two Regimes of Madness: Texts and Interviews 1975–1995*, trans. Ames Hodges and Mike Taormina (New York: Semiotext(e), 2007), p. 141.
8. Maurice Merleau-Ponty, *World of Perception*, trans. Oliver Davis (London: Routledge, 2004). Sartre's radio shows have not yet been compiled into a single volume; see Alys Moody, '"Conquering the Virtual Public": Jean-Paul Sartre's *La tribune des temps modernes* and the Radio in France', in Matthew Feldman, Erik Tonning and Henry Mead (eds), *Broadcasting in the Modernist Era* (London: Bloomsbury Academic, 2015), pp. 245–65. A useful overview of this rich archive is to be found in the compilation in six CDs of some of these interviews in *Anthologie sonore de la pensée française par les philosophes du XXe siècle* (Paris: Fremeaux, 2002), or the recent book series *Audiographie* published by éditions EHESS.
9. Jean-François Lyotard, *The Postmodern Explained to Children*, trans. Don Barry, Bernadette Maher, Julian Pefanis, Virginia Spate and Morgan Thomas (Minneapolis: University of Minnesota Press, 1992), p. 100.
10. Stiegler together with his association Ars Industrialis created their own podcast between October 2008 and June 2012 to broadcast their

talks and debates. See <http://arsindustrialis.org/podcast.xml> (last accessed 14 September 2016).

11. In response to his critics who accuse him of setting up a nineteenth-century-style philosophical system, Stiegler writes that his repetitions are meant 'in the same way that maps may be used to take stock' and to 'write a new chapter in an adventure begun a long time ago'. Bernard Stiegler, *Symbolic Misery, Vol. 2: The Catastrophe of the Sensible*, trans. Barnaby Norman (Cambridge: Polity Press, 2015), pp. 1–2.

12. Pierre Macherey, 'En matérialiste (1981)', in *Histoires de dinosaure: Faire de la philosophie 1965–1997* (Paris: Presses Universitaires de France, 1999), pp. 96–9.

13. See p. 86.

14. Jean-Louis Fabiani, *Qu'est-ce qu'un philosophe français? La vie sociale des concepts (1880–1980)* (Paris: Éditions EHESS, 2010), p. 18.

15. 'Handless writing is perhaps what we are doing now as we record our voices.' Jacques Derrida, *Paper Machine*, trans. Rachel Bowlby (Stanford: Stanford University Press, 2005), p. 21.

16. See Hervé Glevarec, *France Culture à l'oeuvre: Dynamique des professions et mise en forme radiophonique* (Paris: CNRS éditions, 2001); Patrick Broguière, *France Culture: La destruction programmée d'une université populaire* (Paris: Les Éditions Delga, 2007); Anne-Marie Autissier, 'France-Culture: Rôle et programmation d'une radio à vocation culturelle', PhD dissertation in sociology, University of Paris 5 Descartes, 1997, and the special issue on 'France Culture: A French Singularity', *Le Débat*, 95 (May–August 1997).

17. Jean-Louis Jeanney, 'France-Culture', in Lawrence D. Kritzman (ed.), *The Columbia History of Twentieth-Century French Thought* (New York: Columbia University Press, 2006), pp. 703–6.

18. Some useful documents on the evolution of France Culture, especially in the late 1990s and early 2000s, can be found on the 'Défense de France Culture' website: <http://ddfc.free.fr> (last accessed 14 September 2016).

19. Adèle Van Reeth, 'Actualité de la philosophie', *Strass de la philosophie* (blog), 12 February 2015, <http://strassdelaphilosophie.blogspot.co.uk/2015/02/actualite-de-la-philosophie-adele-van.html> (last accessed 14 September 2016).

20. See p. 61.

21. 'At the very origin and up until now, philosophy has repressed technics as an object of thought. Technics is the unthought.' Bernard

Stiegler, *Technics and Time, Vol. 1: The Fault of Epimetheus*, trans. Richard Beardsworth and George Collins (Stanford: Stanford University Press, 1998), p. ix.

22. 'Much before the hypertext and electronics, an entire *retentional* and *virtual* space, static but perfectly operative, physically surrounds [*encadre*] the writer working at her/his desk. Subtle techniques of annotation, correlation and classification organise from the very origin the writing of works [*œuvres*], that can now be transposed to the domain of the digital media for the benefit of the reader-scribe: these works have become incommensurably *dynamised*.' Bernard Stiegler, 'Machines à écrires et matières à penser', *Genesis. Revue internationale de critique génétique*, 5 (1994), <http://www.iri.centrepompidou.fr/documents/MACHINES_A_ECRIRE_ET_MATIERES_A_PENSER_1994.doc> (last accessed 14 September 2016).

23. Technics here are to be understood as instruments or tools but also techniques, in Marcel Mauss's sense of 'techniques of the body' that Stiegler sometimes refers to. See Bernard Stiegler, 'La lutherie électronique et la main du pianiste', *Cahiers du Centre International de Recherches en Esthétique Musicale/Collège International de Philosophie* (Mont-Saint-Aignan: Institut de musicologie, 1989), p. 234.

24. Stiegler, *Acting Out*, p. 16.

25. Bernard Stiegler, *Pharmacologie du Front national* (Paris: Flammarion, 2013), p. 131.

26. The expression 'becoming-philosopher' was used by Stiegler to refer to this conversion in the 2003 conference 'Acting Out' (*Passer à l'acte*), which was contemporary to the radio interviews published here. This was discussed in response to Marianne Alphant's question 'how does one become a philosopher in the intimacy and the secret of one's life?', referring implicitly to Stiegler's secret, his incarceration in Toulouse between 1978 and 1983. See Stiegler, *Acting Out*, p. 1, pp. 10–11.

27. Stiegler always comes back to the etymology of *thesis* as 'position'. This probably explains the recurrence of the term 'position' in works of French philosophy (for example, *Positions* is the title of at least two books, one by Derrida in 1972 and one by Althusser in 1976).

28. Jean Laplanche and Jean-Bertrand Pontalis, *The Language of Psycho-Analysis*, trans. Donald Nicholson-Smith (London: Karnac Books, 1973), pp. 111–14.

29. Ian James, *The New French Philosophy* (Cambridge: Polity Press, 2012), pp. 61–82.

30. A transductive relation is a relation that constitutes the terms.
31. Stiegler, *Acting Out*, p. 19.
32. Bernard Stiegler, 'Derrida and Technics: Fidelity at the Limits of Deconstruction and the Prosthesis of Faith', in Tom Cohen (ed.), *Jacques Derrida and the Humanities: A Critical Reader* (Cambridge: Cambridge University Press, 2002), p. 246. Here *eidos* refers to the essence of the object, broadly equivalent to the Platonic Idea.
33. Bernard Stiegler, *Technics and Time, Vol. 3: Cinematic Time and the Question of Malaise*, trans. Stephen Barker (Stanford: Stanford University Press, 2011), pp. 40–73.
34. Victor Petit has written an insightful glossary of some of these concepts. See 'Vocabulaire d'Ars Industrialis', in Stiegler, *Pharmacologie du Front national*, pp. 369–441.
35. Stiegler, *Acting Out*, p. 33.
36. Serge Trottein, 'Technics, or the Fading Away of Aesthetics', in Christina Howells and Gerald Moore (eds), *Stiegler and Technics* (Edinburgh: Edinburgh University Press, 2013), p. 95. Trottein calls Stiegler an illusionist, a magician or even a manipulator, and his philosophy a slide show or a cinema.
37. Bernard Stiegler, *Technics and Time, Vol. 2: Disorientation*, trans. Stephen Barker (Stanford: Stanford University Press, 2008), pp. 177–80.
38. See Jean-François Lyotard, '*Logos* and *Techne*, or Telegraphy', in *The Inhuman: Reflections on Time*, trans. Geoffrey Bennington and Rachel Bowlby (Cambridge: Polity Press, 1991), pp. 47–57; Bernard Stiegler, *States of Shock: Stupidity and Knowledge in the Twenty-First Century*, trans. Daniel Ross (Cambridge: Polity Press, 2015), pp. 96–9. For a comparative study of Lyotard and Stiegler on technics, see Ashley Woodward, *Lyotard and the Inhuman Condition: Reflections on Nihilism, Information and Art* (Edinburgh: Edinburgh University Press, 2016), particularly chapter 3.
39. Jean-François Lyotard, 'Enframing of Art. *Epokhe* of Communication', in *Textes dispersés 1: Esthétique et théorie de l'art/Miscellaneous Texts 1: Aesthetics and Theory of Art*, ed. Herman Parret, trans. Vlad Ionescu, Erica Harris and Peter W. Wilne (Leuven: Leuven University Press, 2012), pp. 176–93. For instance, he calls for 'new "*epokhal*" communities, new practices of the *epokhe*, that are necessarily instrumental (the technicisation of *teckne* is thus not in itself the problem)' (p. 193).
40. Stiegler, *Technics and Time, Vol. 2*, p. 30.
41. See the excellent article by Javier de la Higuera, 'Paris et les montagnes, au sommets du monde: Sur l'ontologie événementielle', in Benoît Dillet

and Alain Jugnon (eds), *Technologiques: La Pharmacie de Bernard Stiegler* (Nantes: Cécile Defaut, 2013), pp. 167–87.

42. See in particular: Geoffrey Bennington, 'Emergencies', in *Interrupting Derrida* (London: Routledge, 2000), pp. 162–79; Tracy Colony, 'Epimetheus Bound: Stiegler on Derrida, Life, and the Technological Condition', *Research in Phenomenology*, 41 (2011), pp. 72–89; Nathan Van Camp, 'Negotiating the Anthropological Limit: Derrida, Stiegler, and the Question of the Animal', *Between the Species: An Online Journal for the Study of Philosophy and Animals*, 14.1 (2011), pp. 57–80; Ben Turner, 'Life and the Technical Transformation of *Différance*: Stiegler and the Noo-Politics of Becoming Non-Inhuman', *Derrida Today*, forthcoming.

43. Personal communication with Élie During, 5 June 2015.

44. Jacques Rancière, *The Emancipated Spectator*, trans. Gregory Elliott (London: Verso, 2008), p. 46.

45. Richard Beardsworth, 'Technology and Politics: A Response to Bernard Stiegler', *Cultural Politics*, 6.2 (2010), pp. 181–99, partially reprinted in Howells and Moore (eds), *Stiegler and Technics*, pp. 208–24.

46. Stiegler, *Technics and Time, Vol. 3*, p. 81.

47. Jean-François Lyotard, *Why Philosophize?*, trans. Andrew Brown (Cambridge: Polity Press, 2013).

48. 'Our answer is this: you will not evade desire, the law of presence-absence, the law of the debt, you will find no refuge, not even in action.' Lyotard, *Why Philosophize?*, p. 122.

49. Bernard Stiegler, *Taking Care of Youth and the Generations*, trans. Stephen Barker (Stanford: Stanford University Press, 2010), p. 107.

50. Stiegler, *Taking Care*, p. 109.

51. See the third part, 'The Pharmacology of the Question', in Bernard Stiegler, *What Makes Life Worth Living*, trans. D. Ross (Cambridge: Polity Press, 2013), pp. 99–133.

52. The last sentence of *Technics and Time, Vol. 1* reads as a promise and aide-mémoire for the next volumes: 'Whence the excess of measure in this exceptional phrase inscribed on the wall of time: *no future.*' Stiegler, *Technics and Time, Vol. 1*, p. 276.

53. Stiegler, *What Makes Life Worth Living*, p. 108.

54. 'Political individuation is regulated by a legislation founded on the possibility and the duty to interpret the law, since the law makes up a preindividual found charged with potential that is fundamentally jurisprudential. In other words, political individuation is constituted by a hermeneutic jurisprudence.' Bernard Stiegler, *La Société automatique,*

Vol. 1: L'Avenir du travail (Paris: Fayard, 2015), p. 260. Further on, Stiegler reminds us that the very young Marx, who first studied law, 'wanted to make jurisprudence the true philosophy' (p. 282).

55. Laurent de Sutter, *Deleuze: La Pratique du droit* (Paris: Michalon, 2009), p. 66.

56. Gilles Deleuze, *Francis Bacon: The Logic of Sensation*, trans. Daniel W. Smith (London: Continuum, 2004), p. 125.

Philosophising by Accident

Interviews with Élie During

1. Philosophy and Technics

Élie During (ÉD): Bernard Stiegler, the expression 'philosophy of technics', often used to describe your work, is exact yet perhaps insufficient. It is exact since the three volumes that you have published these last ten years as part of the series Technics and Time *are indeed books of philosophy, and their main object is technics:* The Fault of Epimetheus *was first published in 1994, followed by* Disorientation *in 1996, and more recently, in 2001,* Cinematic Time and the Question of Malaise. *It is also insufficient since 'philosophy of technics' does not account for the atypical relation that you maintain with the philosophical institution. At the moment, you are director of the Institut de recherche et coordination acoustique/musique (IRCAM), before this position, you were the adjunct general director of the Institut national de l'audiovisuel (INA) for three years, and you have also been teaching for many years now at the University of Compiègne, which is a technological university with its own unique model. Before beginning to teach there, you were the programme director at the Collège internationale de philosophie (Ciph) in Paris.*

Additionally, while not being an engineer yourself, you have always had a very close relation to technics – to technological rationality, to the modes of technical organisation, to both scientific and industrial questions of 'technoscience'. We can see in this a certain necessity for philosophy to maintain a philosophical relation with a non-philosophical outside. But I think that, more deeply for you, it is also a matter of a personal relation to technics – and this is my first question: how did you arrive, not only to philosophy of technics, but to technics itself?

Bernard Stiegler (BS): I indeed began being interested in technics for itself and not only as a philosophical object long before becoming a philosopher with an interest in technics. I expressed an interest in technics and technologies *long before* turning to philosophy. I've always had this spontaneous interest, this inclination and this curiosity for technical objects. They always appeared to me as a kind of mystery. This perhaps explains why in some of the oldest societies, technics and magic are one and the same, while in Greece, *technē* is both the possibility of excessive-ness [*démesure*], the famous *ubris*, as well as what we today call art.

I suppose this inclination comes from several factors that I cannot fully refer to here – and without doubt the main ones have slipped my mind. Among other things that appear to me as the most striking and significant is this one: I am first the son of Robert Stiegler, a technician and electronics engineer, who initiated me from a very young age to these technical and technological questions, for which I later expressed a great passion. It is without doubt this admiration for my father that led me to read, long before my teenage years, a short book for the general public which was also used by my father, if I remember well: the title was *La radio, mais c'est très simple!* [*Radio, there is nothing easier!*], and it was published before the war. I learned about the operating of valves, pentodes and others as well as the functioning of transformers, elements, condensers, amplifiers, beat frequency oscillators (BFOs), etc. In short, I was introduced to everything from the invisible world of elec-trons used to produce and receive electromagnetic waves. I met these electronic tubes again only thirty years later, in the work of Gilbert Simondon and the morphodynamic analyses. Then I began making small electronic circuits such as balances, oscillators and small ensem-bles of objects with the components that I got from my father. I was doing this at a time before the introduction of integrated circuits and micro-electronics, but after the time of electronic tubes. I was around twelve years old.

The role that I have given to technics in my thought was influ-enced by the materialist vision of the politico-philosophical thing that I adopted in secondary school at a very young age. I joined the French Communist Party (PCF) after 1968 when many decided to leave it for other groups on the Left. The path I took was in the reverse direction: I went from the extreme left-wing *groupuscules* to those whom I, with my comrades, called 'the Stalinians', mostly because this popular party claimed a philosophical framework to guide its actions. A thought of the 'modes of production' was inscribed at the heart of the Party's theory. I deeply admired what I believed then to be the project of allowing each and every one to think as part of a formal consideration and a collective theorisation: from the point of view of a philosophy exposed to both public criticism [*critique publique*] and the course of things, in other words, from the thought of work and production. I admired the existence of *Nouvelle Critique*,[1] where we could read Lacan rereading Freud, debating structuralism and Barthes, and that Picasso was loved by so many workers.

Even though later on I left the Communist Party together with its superficial materialist view, I continue to consider myself a materialist. But I see in ordinary materialism an archaic and vulgar form of metaphysics. I continue to belong to those who believe – after Marx – that instruments of production play a decisive role in the mode of human living. And of course, I've always thought that these very instruments of production were above all technical organs. Yet I do not think that Marx allows us to go far enough with this question, precisely because he fails to think the complex relation between technics and time even when he conceives in an essential way modern technics as a measure of time. My current relation to philosophy is deeply affected by this Marxian question of technics but also by this second question that is closely linked to it: *praxis* as a practice of thought, as well as a thought in and of practice.

In my properly philosophical story, which started relatively late, and somewhat by accident,[2] I did not first question technics but memory and, through Plato, *anamnesis* as the possibility of knowing and as the origin of knowledge itself (what is called in a Kantian language the conditions of possibility of experience). Besides, I continue to believe that there is no other possible way to *arrive at* philosophy than by questioning the origin of knowledge, which also constitutes the very possibility of knowledge.

It was on this path of memory that I found 'technics': I realised much later that technics was in fact at the heart of the philosophical question of memory. I do not consider myself a 'philosopher of technics', but rather a philosopher who contributes with others in establishing that the philosophical question *is*, and is *through and through*, the endurance of a condition that I call techno-logical: both technical and logical, always already forged on the cross that forms language and tools, that is, that allows the *externalisation* [*extériorisation*] of the human.

In my work, I attempt to show that, ever since its origin, philosophy encounters [*fait épreuve*] this techno-logical condition, *but by repressing and disavowing technology*. Such is the difficulty of my enterprise: to show that *philosophy begins in repressing its own question*. To put it differently, my ambition is to take the philosophical question to its roots. I think that today this is possible – not because I am the chosen one (or the damned) to execute this mission, but because our contemporary times call for it. Today we live in the time of technology, which emerged from the

Industrial Revolution, and so the question of technics is raised anew, as everyone can now perceive.

However, the history of metaphysics as well as the quasi-totality of academic philosophy is marked by the ignorance of this question. Due to this ignorance, a large part of academic philosophy therefore remains abstract and isolated from the becoming of the world; it is cut off from the world.

The fact that, from Plato onwards, the relation between philosophy and technics manifests itself essentially, originally and durably as a conflict is only one part of the story. Indeed, after the nineteenth century, the situation becomes more complex: with industrialisation, technics comes closer to science (and becomes technology *sensu stricto*), and the world composed of those we now call 'the intellectuals' distances itself from technics that turned into technology, from science, from economy, and, eventually, from political economy.

This established relation – or, to be more precise, this non-relation – is terrible: of course one can find exceptions; the picture is not all dark. At the end of the twentieth century and at the beginning of this twenty-first century, we can often hear philosophers say, either with fright or with complacency, with an enjoyment close to that of Mr Homais in *Madame Bovary*, 'Personally, I have *never* understood a thing about technics', which is another way to claim 'and I will *never do anything* to understand it even a little'. 'I have a computer and a mobile phone, and I *absolutely don't* understand how they function': we often hear this, expressing self-gratitude which is entirely stupid and, to some degree, miserable. As if we could ever feel proud of *not understanding* how a system functions. How can we claim to understand anything about Hegel if we do not feel capable of understanding the functioning of a diode? Hegel, who himself wrote on electricity, would have undoubtedly found this ludicrous.[3] Technics and technology are often subject to these kinds of clichés, although of course at times they are expressed in a more sophisticated manner, but nonetheless for me they appear as *small symptoms* (as Freud speaks of 'small differences') of the disavowal and repression of the question of technics – which is itself the originary question of philosophical thought. Philosophy has never ceased to think technics in the negative form (and maybe, without knowing it, as the negative per se, or even as the negative of the negative – in all the diverse senses that this word can have). But its non-thought becomes today both evident and manifestly desolating; it is the sign of a tragic powerlessness [*impuis-*

sance], if not a great impertinence, that sometimes takes a hysterical and perfectly untenable shape.

Amongst these clichés, there is a firm belief that knowledge of the functioning of an automobile motor is not required in order to know how to drive it, and, more generally, that we do not need to know what is happening in technics to know how to think. Yet this cliché overlooks the question of knowing what it means *to drive*. Obviously, one can get into one's car to drive just like any other driver on a Sunday, and this is how I personally drive. But to really drive is not only this. Driving an automobile, regardless of one's use, requires to account for its full capacities: whether one can drive, for instance, at 250 kph with a vehicle without breaking this vehicle and killing oneself. This phantasm of speed and power is without a doubt responsible for many accidents and behaviours that are intolerable and degrading for those behaving this way – these consumers of the automobile industry are highly representative of the contemporary degradation of all being-together [*être-ensemble*]. But precisely, besides thinking of driving *as a way to produce phantasms*, driving at the limits of the machine should also be thought independently of these phantasmic dimensions. The machine is primarily the opening of new possibles, and it is always in relation to this opening that it is in use – even for those who, like me and like most people, live in the mediocre average of those possibles. To put it differently, thinking 'driving' is knowing that driving also includes the possibility of carrying the machine to its limits and therefore, one way or another, *being familiar* with these limits *in theory*. Consequently, one should know what happens *in the motor*.

To philosophise is always, one way or another, 'to carry the machine to its limits', and this should be understood not only metaphorically. To philosophise is always to desire to go to the limits of questions – to their originary limits, that is, to the root of questions. Radical thinking intends to uncover the root of things, and during my own philosophical journey I thought I found technics *as this root*. And with it, the machine.

Rather than taking questions by their roots, we can take them by their ends (by their purposes [*motifs*], these last extremities). We can argue, like Aristotle, that the end is already contained in the origin. In this sense, conducting a radical analysis of what constitutes the origin of a being also tells us something about its end, since, after all, both the origin and the end make up the essence of this being – what makes it identical across time. To use reason this way is to miss the problem of

Is it because technics affects our thought?

time and becoming (besides, time does not only equate to becoming). Contrary to Aristotle and to all metaphysics – to all 'onto-theology', as we call it after Heidegger – I believe that an accidental process takes place *between the origin and the end; we cannot speak only of an essential process for there are occurrences that disturb the metaphysical illusion that the end is already there in the origin. Philosophy should learn how to think this accidentality (together with its genealogy).*

Yet this accidentality is precisely the first sense of technics – which I also refer to as prostheticity. We can attempt to think this way with Aristotle as well: the 'prime unmoved mover' (God) is for him the end as *motive* [*motif*], that is, reason (of all things). Therefore, the *movement*, and the *accidental journey* [*parcours*] that it consists in, would be what counts the most, together with the *traces* produced, since the mover is accidental (accidents are at the origin of scars that are traces and marks) and these traces are also linked as *traumas*, *phantasms* and *fetishes* to the 'prime motor' that is the determinant of *desire*.

ÉD: We are now in metaphysics. But we are also about to break the circle that it makes together with its critique – without having to produce a difficult critique of critique. By following you, it would seem that we need to radically raise the problems, but only once we have changed our mind about what 'radical', 'the origin' and 'originary' mean. Yet, you explained that a radical thought could only go to its limits by interrogating the limits of the machine, by carrying the technical dispositive to its limits – instead of tracing in an a priori manner the split between the mechanical and what exceeds it, or envisaging the meaning of technics only in relation to the essential or constitutive role it plays in the destiny of metaphysics. This idea or demand for a radical thought is striking in your work. It is as if your books are marked by a tension between this singular interest that you have in technics and what traditional philosophy pretends to say about it. Behind technics as a fact, there is what technics does and what is at stake concretely: in your view, this is what it means to think. Yet, paradoxically, this concern is translated in your writing as a certain technicity or technicality that is not linked to the specificity of the vocabulary of technics itself, but to a properly philosophical technicality. There is a rigour in the conceptual elaboration, the necessity of reworking concepts and therefore using language itself to displace and recover certain problems, but in a radical way. This comes into play concretely in the invention or the borrowing of neologisms (earlier you mentioned 'prostheticity'), but also in your close dialogues with Husserl's phenomenology, in your commentary on On the Phenomenology of the Consciousness of Internal Time,[4] *or the rereading of* Critique of Pure Reason *and the three syntheses of the 'Transcendental Analytics', or in the play of constant references to the Greek tradition, to the Heideggerian analyses, etc. A superficial reading would give the impression of a 'hyperphilosophical' approach that, in order to push the limits of technics, would have to re-interrogate the history and the foundation of the entire philosophical tradition. The question that should then be raised is how it is possible to relate to technics, its singularities and its accidental nature, while producing at the same time a discourse that is much more classically philosophical than for instance Simondon, who wanted to follow the internal dialectic of technics by cultivating a certain distrust regarding all things that could take the shape of a 'philosophising' philosophy of technics. Maybe this is not a paradox, but this first image allows us to get a better sense of how these two threads are tied in your work: the interest in technics and the work of philosophical memory.*

BS: I am interested in grounding again and *entirely* the question of technics. Entirely, since I consider the philosophical question is the question of technics. I do not write a philosophy of technics like those who write on the philosophy of art, moral philosophy or political philosophy, as regions of knowledge belonging to a broader and more general philosophical knowledge. Technics for me is not a regional object, but a philosophical object in itself. I raise the question of technics *as* the philosophical question, and *from this point of view* I am in a hyperphilosophy. I attempt to elaborate once again, and *in full*, the philosophical question, and therefore to revisit in the most general way the founding concepts of philosophical thought in their entirety, but always on the basis of the technical question. I consider this project an uncovering of a *forgotten* origin of all these questions, and also my question is what I call the *default of origin*. This is what leads me to readings that are technical, philosophically speaking. Lately I undertook very close line-by-line readings of Kant, at the moment I am reading Plato again, and in the past it was Heidegger and Husserl.

Yet these reading experiences are often, and maybe even always, founded directly or indirectly on technical or technological *experiences*. Questions about prehistory had as much of a crucial role in my thought as works on extremely recent technologies, undertaken at the university of Compiègne. I organised there, around 1992, a seminar that joined these questions; it was called 'From the Flint to the Hypertext', and it was intended for an audience specialised in artificial intelligence. My research into prehistory led to a collaboration with a team that was close to the palaeoanthropologist André Leroi-Gourhan. This team conducted what is known as experimental technology: reconstituting in a laboratory the gestures of carving a flint and, with these gestures, gaining access to human worlds (in this specific case, the Neanderthal world). These sorts of things led to a problematisation of technics from an anthropological point of view, and this has partly fed into the ideas I developed in *Technics and Time, Vol. 1: The Fault of Epimetheus*, when I was attempting a new reading of Heidegger's *Being and Time*. But I also undertook, around the same time, research on digital technology applied to the text when I conducted the exhibition *Memories of the Future* at the Georges Pompidou Centre in 1987. Around 1990, I worked on a system of computer-assisted reading with the Bibliothèque nationale de France, in collaboration with the University of Compiègne. I drew on these works when I wrote *Technics and Time, Vol. 2: Disorientation*.

But this is also true for the book on Kant, *Technics and Time, Vol. 3: Cinematic Time and the Question of Malaise*, which was conceived when I was directing the Institut national de l'audiovisuel (INA). This position allowed me to think the industrial problems linked to television, digitisation and cultural industries, and the relation between television and society. This forced me to problematise the politics of industry, the role of politics vis-à-vis cultural industries, and to confront the emerging technoscientific problems linked to the future of images in their digital form. To think thoroughly the future of images requires us to revisit the Kantian question of the schematism and the three syntheses of imagination.

ÉD: But, once again, how can we make sure that this radical questioning of technics does not entirely fall back into questioning the relation of philosophy itself with technics, and therefore producing more philosophy from philosophy? You mentioned the significance of technical experiences for thinking technics. But philosophers are lazy, like everyone; they do not always want to take the time to really learn about technics. Some even feel a form of paradoxical enjoyment in not getting interested in technics; they even sometimes consider this lack of knowledge of the workings of machines (a computer or a fax machine) as a sign of distinction. This behaviour is perhaps encouraged by the university-based habitus. Beyond the anecdotal, this brings us back to the interesting problem of the philosophy symptom regarding technics: this tension or complex has been expressed ever since the origin of philosophy, and has revealed itself at times more violently than other times, by repressing technē itself in all its forms. This problem was raised in the twentieth century with Heidegger, for example, who envisaged a radical thought of technics only from the history of being, and he was therefore condemned to miss the specific determination of technics, in their diversity.

BS: In a certain way, the process of repressing the question of technics by philosophy has increased all the more today, now that we live in an outburst of technical forces, an outburst of 'impersonal forces', using Blanchot's terms. Reactive forces produce this outburst; I refer to 'reactive' in Nietzsche's sense, which strangely echoes the motto of 'being reactive' used by managers in private companies. This extraordinary acceleration of technical development, which has become technological, produces today, in the totality of the world's population, a feeling of huge disorientation.

Yet I believe that if we want to evaluate this contemporary situation of disorientation – and how, by becoming technology, technics plays a dominant role – the birth of philosophy should be reinterpreted from the point of view of the appearance of technicity in Greek thought. It is worth noting that this question is particularly an Athenian question, and that by 'birth of philosophy' I mean the appearance of Plato as a figure.

Plato is the one who makes Socrates, his master, speak. In my view, Socrates is not yet part of philosophy – he is there at the beginning, but he is still in what *is not yet* philosophy: he remains a *tragic*, he is standing in between the tragic era and the philosophical one. On this particular point, I believe that Nietzsche made a mistake. To put it differently, Socrates is still very close to the pre-Socratics, the poet-thinkers who are above all *city-state founders*. It is crucial to note that these first tragic thinkers are jurists as well as poets, and they expressed themselves *poetically* and produced this singular experience of language for an *essential* reason: it is from this poetry that they think the foundation of their city-states, while also being concerned by the simplicity of geometrical evidence – they are mathematicians, geometricians, as much as poets.

In the case of Socrates, we can never affirm with enough strength and resonance that he claims an experience of the shaman that is constantly occulted by Plato (except in the wonderful dialogue *Symposium*). He is by himself a turning point in history.

Philosophy *sensu stricto* is Plato, manifestly inspired by Plato; unlike Nietzsche, who believed that Socrates led to the exit from the tragic era, I believe that it is Plato who made this gesture, at the same time that he occulted Socrates' thought. Philosophy then begins both in this withdrawal [*effacement*] and in the condemnation of technics identified as sophism: it is, however, one and the same gesture.

One of the great tasks of our time remains to exhume Socrates' speech from its burying by metaphysics, which was born with Plato.[5]

Philosophy began as metaphysics – and for me, metaphysics is an originary occultation that leads the critical position to ineluctably turn sour,
much like milk – in a dogmatism grounded on simple oppositions, by
reducing the elementary complexity where *the element is not only 'simple'*
precisely because it is always already 'supplementary',[6] that is, technical,
or 'prosthetic'.[7]

Plato and philosophy appeared at a time of deep crisis in the Greek
city-state. During this time, sophists appeared, and these figures embodied the essence of the crisis (but this crisis cannot only be reduced to
them; there are, of course, many other elements to take into consideration, such as monetary factors). According to Plato, with sophists,
the idle talk of those who know everything reigned; they were 'poly-
maths' (or polytechnicians[8]) to whom Socrates soon opposed his non-
knowledge, his default of knowledge from which Diotima, in *Symposium*,
draws the very principle of philosophy as love and gift of what she does
not have: knowledge.

The Greek city-state, emerging between the seventh and sixth centuries BC, transfers the *polemos* of arms to language itself: the conflictual
relations between individuals become relations of language, and they
are played out (as much as possible) in the universe of symbols. The city-
state is the takeover of the human community by *logos*: it is a real passion
for *logos*, speech as an experience of thought, and a thought that is intrinsically tied to the question of collective decision. Thought is therefore
essentially, as a passionate experience of speech, and even when it is a
geometrical speech, the thought of *being-togetherness* [*l'être ensemble*].

We cannot understand anything of this period if we forget that Thales
practises geometry while founding a city-state, and that all this was only
possible thanks to a fundamental and primordial passion for language,
which was first of all poetic language (and, against all expectations, logic
proceeds from this poetics; this is what Parmenides means). As Jean-
Pierre Vernant has taught us, this poetic language was closely linked to
its writing: the alphabet that we continue to use today was invented at
that time.

From Thales to Socrates, Greece was in the tragic era, producing Hesiod's poetry, Aeschylus' great tragedy, the pre-Socratics and
Sophocles. But, at the end of these two centuries, a crisis took place, and
it was from this crisis that the figure of the sophist emerged. Finding the
path of a new truth (that is, a good decision) in the experience of language was less central to the sophist than using the language with skill,

as a device of domination to control the spirits of the city-state, to seize power in the city-state (with an *effective* decision). Here, the poeticity of language, in this case rhetoric, became a technicity of the *pithanon*: the force of persuasion, the control of the *doxa*, the manipulation of public opinion.

Plato and Socrates identify this change that occurred in speech as a technicisation of language and thought, but they also perceive in this technicisation a destruction. For the philosopher, the technician who undoubtedly has knowledge – that we now call 'know-how' or *savoir-faire* but that the Greeks at that time called *technē* – cannot explain this know-how. The sophist only had a kind of false knowledge that generated shams [*faux-semblants*], even though it appeared as real knowledge due to its efficiency. This real knowledge was considered dangerous given its limitlessness and excessiveness [*démesure*] and self-confidence – the famous *hubris*. Even though it was *real*, it could not have been *true* since it was *unlimited*.

However, *hubris* haunted the city-state long before the sophists; it is at the very heart of the tragic experience (and it is still at the heart of Sophocles' *Oedipus the King*). *Hubris* was without a doubt, for Greek tragedy, irreducibly there as a destiny or as an originary condition that needed to be contained but that could not be avoided. With Plato and philosophy, the question of excessiveness becomes the question of technics, artifice in general, *mimēsis*, art, poetry and music, since, to him, all this belonged to the technical *savoir-faire* (this leads him to condemn the poetic language of the pre-Socratics). And to be overcome, this immoderation [*démesure*] needed to be subjected to a moderation [*mesure*]: *the moderation of the Idea.*

ÉD: It is therefore the excessiveness of language that disquiets philosophy and puts it in danger. Yet this is also translated paradoxically as a possibility to enrol and instrumentalise language . . .

BS: Once the sophists seized language, such an excessiveness turned language into the milieu of *insignificance*, the overwhelming ordinary *idle talk* finally leading to scepticism, disappointment and cynicism. This was not a moment in philosophy but the sinking of the common (what is the most precious for the city-state) into vanity. At the beginning of the Greek experience of speech, at the beginning of the *polis*, language was on the contrary the experience of discovery, the famous wonder that

Aristotle would later raise as the philosophical posture par excellence, but also of affect and knowledge, that is above all the *desire* for knowledge and knowledge as the essential fruit of desire, a knowledge which is in a way delightful [*savoureux*].[9]

The technical question was raised this way at the origin of philosophy, with Plato's discourse: in denouncing a sophistic becoming of speech. But, in fact, it was not presented as the technical question *as such*. It was presented both as a question of rhetoric, in denouncing the rhetorical usage of language by the sophist (particularly in *Gorgias*), and, above all, as the question that Plato calls *hypomnesis*, that is, the technical memory.[10]

Hypomnesis means 'artificial memory'. Yet anyone who studied even a little philosophy in secondary school would know that the great Platonic question is that of reminiscence, or, in Greek, *anamnesis*. They would have also heard of the famous dialogue, *Meno*, in which Socrates discusses with a young Athenian slave (Meno): Meno is on his way to a class given by a sophist, where he hopes to learn 'to be virtuous'. Socrates interrupts his walk and roughly tells him this: 'Are you sure that it is worth your time and your money to go listen to a sophist telling you what is virtue? Before getting there, let us try first, you and I, to think together, by our-selves and without any "generally accepted idea", without pretending to know *already* what virtue is, without claiming any knowledge, and even in affirming a non-knowledge, let us make an effort to dialogue, in other words to use dialectics, to think together *what is* virtue.'

Meno, who is honest and respectable, agrees to participate in this exercise and suggests examples of virtue through examples of virtuous people.[11] But Socrates tells him that precisely every time that he takes the part for the whole, that is, he reduces virtue to one of these cases, on the contrary the unity of these cases should be found. This unity cannot be an empirical example and, in all logic, it should therefore *precede* the diversity of all the possible cases of virtue. To put it differently, *virtue* (the unity of all the cases of being virtuous) is not a reality that can be found by itself in experience. Hence, *it is about searching for what cannot be found in experience*: searching for an a priori essence. The discourse on being and its essences, or ontology, is invented in this manner; it constitutes the basis of – what Kant calls in the eighteenth century – the transcendental.

Socrates puts forward his method (dialectics) to attempt to find *what is* virtue, that is, to define the essence of virtue. All of a sudden, Meno interrupts him to say something along these lines: 'But my dear Socrates, you are not in earnest. There are two possibilities: either you do not know what virtue is and, if such a thing is possible and we find it, you will not recognise it. You will let it pass by without knowing that you found it. Or, in the case that you will in fact recognise it, this means that you had known it already. Therefore, you were not really looking for it. You were pretending to search for it.' This is an extraordinary and famous aporia; it is known in the philosophical tradition as Meno's aporia, and it gives expression to the radical scepticism that many sophists used.

I believe that it is in front of this aporia that Socrates recognises the true dimension of thinking (since we begin to think from this sceptical moment), but also the most dangerous dimension of thinking: if we allow ourselves to remain in this sceptical moment, we cease to think even before having really started to think. We need to find the resources to overcome this moment. In front of this power of thought that can make thought powerless, Socrates answers with a myth. He introduces the myth of Persephone:[12] 'You are right, Meno, your discourse is entirely coherent and I cannot be against what you have just said. In fact, if I recognise virtue, this means that I already knew it: I knew it *in a previous life*, but I *have forgotten it.' Anamnesis* is in fact a recognition.

Later on, in *Phaedrus*, Plato made Socrates say that his soul, in this previous life, did not have a body – also was even less surrounded by prostheses or artifices – and therefore had a direct contact with truth. Instead, the soul has forgotten everything when falling on Earth, into the body (*soma*) that is also *sema*, the prison. The original fall of the soul into the body is also the fall of the knowledge of essences (and the unity of being that they make up) into the world of becoming and multiplicity, the world of matter and therefore the world of passion and corruption. The opposition between the soul and the body begins.

It should be emphasised that the world of becoming is the world of technics, for the Greeks. The philosopher reproached technics for expressing the ineluctable development of the unstable and contingent becoming, while he himself is searching for the world of stability, being, ideal identities and enduring essences. Plato first discovered in *Meno* the question of *anamnesis*, which designates the remembering [*ressouvenir*] of forgotten essences, awakened by the exercise of dialectics. And in *Phaedrus*, this question is taken up again, but Socrates warns Phaedrus against the dangers of *hypomnesis*, that is, technical or prosthetic memory – a memory that *is aided by writing*. Here, *hypomnesis* is both technics and the cause of oblivion, but it is also the cause of lies and manipulation.

At this point, *aletheia* (truth) and *anamnesis* (reminiscence) become almost synonymous. It is also why Heidegger allowed himself to translate *a-letheia* as 'unconcealedness', 'unconcealment' or 'clearing', translating *a* as the negative of the root *lethe*, 'oblivion'.[13] Truth *is* reminiscence. But forgetfulness engenders lies, and falsehood is the fruit of technics (*hypomnesis*).

In the myth of Epimetheus, told in *Protagoras*, it is striking to observe that, on the contrary, technics comes to the rescue of forgetfulness [*oubli*]. In attempting to oppose the vision of the sophist Protagoras, Plato establishes between *Meno* and *Phaedrus* a chain of correspondences between becoming, technics, oblivion and trickery, opposed to the chain of living memory, being and truth.

This is what leads me to articulate the question of memory and technics and to attempt to rethink the problem of time from this position: to affirm, against Plato, that memory is originally technically constituted.

Notes

1. Monthly review of the French Communist Party.
2. See Bernard Stiegler, 'How I Became a Philosopher', in *Acting Out*, trans. David Barison, Daniel Ross and Patrick Crogan (Stanford: Stanford University Press, 2008), pp. 1–35. At the time that these interviews with Élie During took place, *Acting Out* (first published in 2003) had not yet been published, therefore my philosophical path – which began in the Saint-Michel prison in Toulouse in 1978 – could not have been known. I could not have talked about this in these interviews: it seemed to me indecent to introduce in this setting, through a radiophonic programme and the sensational comments that can come with it, the singular narrative of a philosophical story that is, like all philosophy, intimately existential. Yet this philosophical story, as I have lived it, from its origin until today, is the question of accident, and the acting out [*passage à l'acte*] as accident. I have called this accident ever since 1983, my first interpretation of the myth of Epimetheus, the *default of origin*. This is why, when Élie During and I talked for the first time about this project of interviews, I told him this particular episode of my life, since it seemed impossible not to talk about it, and I also did not hesitate to share this information given the trust that he showed me: this narrative was immediate and with no return. But I also told him that I did not want him to ask during the interviews about the origin of my

relation to philosophy and my practice as a philosopher, but all this is now known. I would have rather explained all this in another setting, when I could have in front of me an audience, who could address me personally. A few weeks later, I gave the conference 'How I Became a Philosopher' at the Centre Georges Pompidou in Paris.

3. While Hegel did not allow for a new thought of technics, nonetheless he asked for the first time the question of exteriority in a way that engendered a new manner of interrogating technics. I inherit this particular point from Hegel.

4. Edmund Husserl, *Collected Works, Vol. 4: On the Phenomenology of the Consciousness of Internal Time* (1893–1917), ed. Rudolf Bernet, trans. John Barnett Brough (Dordrecht: Kluwer Academic Publishers, 1991).

5. I will devote a part of the forthcoming fourth volume of *Technics and Time, Symbols and Diabols, or the War of Spirits,* to this project.

6. I owe this word, this critique of oppositional schemes and many other things to Jacques Derrida.

7. This is not exactly Jacques Derrida's point of view; undoubtedly we diverge on this central point.

8. [Trans.] Stiegler is here referring to the elite French higher education institution for engineering, *École Polytechnique*; students and alumni of this School are called *polytechniciens*.

9. [Trans.] Stiegler is playing on the proximity of *savoir* (knowledge) and *saveur* (savour). Roland Barthes also noted in his Collège de France inaugural lecture in January 1977 that these two words in French share the same Latin root. Roland Barthes, *A Roland Barthes Reader*, ed. Susan Sontag (London: Vintage, 1993), p. 464.

10. On these questions of insignificance and *hypomnesis*, see respectively Stiegler, *Acting Out*, pp. 26–8, 15–16.

11. Plato, 'Meno', in *Meno and Other Dialogues*, trans. Robin Waterfield (Oxford: Oxford University Press, 2005), 79a–80e, pp. 110–13.

12. [Trans.] See Bernard Stiegler, 'Perséphone, Œdipe, Epimethée', *Tekhnema*, 3 (1996), pp. 69–112, and *Technics and Time, Vol. 1: The Fault of Epimetheus*, trans. Richard Beardsworth and George Collins (Stanford: Stanford University Press, 1998), pp. 97–8. Also called *Korē* (the young girl), Persephone is the daughter of Zeus and Demeter in Greek mythology. One day, the God-king of the underworld, Hades, who was enchanted by her, opened the earth and abducted her. From then on, she is said to spend half of the year in the underworld and the rest on earth. Hence the myth of her abduction represents the cycle of

vegetation, coming out for spring and withdrawing in Hades after the harvest (realised by her mother Demeter).

13. [Trans.] Stiegler takes this important element from Heidegger's reading of Plato. See Martin Heidegger, 'Plato's Doctrine of Truth', in *Pathmarks*, trans. Thomas Sheehan (Cambridge: Cambridge University Press, 1998), pp. 155–82. See also Bernard Stiegler, *Technics and Time, Vol. 2: Disorientation*, trans. Stephen Barker (Stanford: Stanford University Press, 2008), pp. 32–5.

2. Technics as Memory

ÉD: After explaining your relation to technics, and more broadly the complex rela-
tion that philosophy has with technics, it might be useful to orient ourselves in your
work by following the central question of trace, inscription and materialised memory.
Continuing with the reference to Meno, Plato *presents through Socrates a demonstra-*
tion of the reminiscence thesis. He allows Meno the slave to rediscover or recollect a
truth by the simple play of the dialogue, or what is also called the dialectical method.
He invites the young slave to find once again the solution to a geometrical problem in
tracing figures in the sand, in other words, to find again in the inscription the trace of a
truth that he had forgotten. Was it the question of trace contained in this dialogue that
led to your own work on technics as memory?

BS: It was indeed by reflecting on this second important moment in
Meno that I began to formulate what was my working hypothesis [*mon*
hypothèse de travail] and became, strictly speaking, a thesis.[1] In this second
moment, Socrates tries to demonstrate that every time I *come to know*
something, I, in fact, recollect it, I find it again in myself and by myself.
This introduces a major thesis: *the only knowledge that exists is produced by*
the one who enunciates it and it can never be received from the outside. Again, this
is the question of the transcendental that was raised some two millen-
nia before the invention of the word (by Kant), but it is above all the
philosophical position par excellence: no idea can be *received*; it should
be *conceived* by the person who inhabits it; *concept* has no other meaning.
In analysing this second moment, I was therefore struck by the role
of drawing and by the necessity of *graphein* ('to inscribe, to write, to
draw') that I formulated in my hypothesis. Plato does not say anything
about *graphein*; he simply accepts it as a given, even though it is *already*
a *hypomnesis*.[2]
   This thesis is my Ariadne's thread in the maze [*dédale*] that I have been
following for the last twenty-five years: memory is always hypomnesic or

technical, even when it is living memory. *Anamnesis* (reminiscence) is always supported and inhabited by a *hypomnesis* (a mnemotechnics), but most of the time this happens in an occult manner since this *hypomnesis* has become 'naturalised': in erasing the technicity, the facticity, the prostheticity and the historicity, and in becoming a 'second nature', memory cannot be perceived – in the same way that a fish cannot see the water, even though it is its *element*.

I am of course here referring to human memory. In conducting the demonstration with a slave, Plato wants to show that every human is potentially a philosophising being – even though most of the time his being is not actually philosophising. I am in complete agreement with Plato on this point. But, contrary to Plato, I believe that we are potentially philosophising to the extent that we are endowed with precisely an artificial memory that supports *the transmission of questions* from generation to generation. This is made possible since it allows the materialisation of time, its spacing and its spatialisation, its preservation, its reactivation, its retemporalisation, its retransmission or its reconstitution, which is also and more generally its re-elaboration and its transformation (what Jacques Derrida calls its *différance*) – through which knowledge 'is progressing' and 'spirit' deploys its historicity. I use 'spirit' here in the sense that knowledge is constituted by a primordial return [*une revenance*]; but I refer also to the materialisation of time as a *condition* of this spirit and, in this sense, I continue to consider myself a materialist. It is undoubtedly an atypical materialism: it is a kind of 'spiritualist' materialism. This 'spiritualist' materialism does not claim that the spirit/mind [*esprit*] is reducible to matter, but that matter is the condition of spirit, in all the nuances of the word 'condition'.

In order to 'reconstitute' or to re-member geometrical reasoning, Meno the slave has *to trace a figure*, that is, to externalise the problem. In my work, I have attempted to show that this necessity of externalisation that seems trivial is already contained in everything that I have said. It is all this content that I have tried to formulate, always in reading and rereading Plato, always coming back to him, and, as I told you earlier, I am currently writing a book on Plato and Socrates. Besides, the title of my Masters dissertation [*maîtrise*] was 'Capitalism, Cybernetics and Textuality'. In this early text, I tried to show that Plato, as the thinker of the head against the body, was the first great thinker of capital (against work, that is, *praxis*), and, paradoxically, he programmed with his metaphysics the cybernetic project, when cybernetics means the science of government,[3] or, in today's vocabulary, management and logistics. He programmed it particularly by trying to eliminate the idiomatic character of language and the corporeality of thought.

Everything that I have written and have published since 1994 is an attempt to introduce a text, of which I wrote a first draft around 1980, and that I reformulated in 1992 as the last part of my doctoral thesis. This text is therefore my starting point and, eventually, the only thing that I am really interested in publishing (and which should become the fifth and last volume of the *Technics and Time* series). I wrote its first version at the time when I was already working on Plato. If I have not yet published it, it is precisely because the four preceding volumes are required to make this last work accessible. This fourth volume is precisely devoted to Plato (but also to Freud and Derrida); all this is due to the fact that my 'discussion' [*explication*][4] with Plato is essential to my goal.

Yet the question that I initially explore in Platonism and the birth of philosophy – memory – only became a question of technics per se, and not only that of *hypomnesis*, when one day I read *Protagoras* and began to meditate a myth narrated by the sophist Protagoras to his friend Socrates. It is the myth of Epimetheus; I believe that the central question of this particular dialogue is to know who can partake in the political decision, and what is political wisdom or knowledge – if there is such a thing.

Protagoras revisits the story of Prometheus and Epimetheus, in a version inspired by both Hesiod and Aeschylus, to support his thesis that anyone can have access to political knowledge. He recounts that one day Zeus asked Prometheus the titan, and Prometheus' twin brother, Epimetheus, to 'bring [the mortal] out into the light of day':[5] animals and ourselves, humans. As Prometheus is set to do this, Zeus decides to give him for this task *dunameis*, 'qualities' or, literally, *potentialities* [*puissances*], which give shape to the unformed clay, giving the light of day to these beings that we are, humans, but also to animals.

Yet Epimetheus asks his brother to let him 'distribute' the *dunameis*, and Prometheus allows his brother. Epimetheus is often distracted and does things all too quickly; he is a kind of rash fool [*gribrouille*] who commits all sorts of stupidities. But he meditates afterwards, and this eventually gives him a form of knowledge: the knowledge of *experience* acquired by those who had a life filled with errors, ended up recognising those errors, and, above all, took time to meditate over them. Eventually they end up becoming 'savants' – as the adjective *epimethes* means in Ancient Greek.

In distributing all the qualities that Zeus confides to him, Epimetheus finally notices that he forgot us, the mortals, those that we call 'humans' (but the Greeks preferred the *mortals*, since they referred to gods as the *immortals*). After giving other species their qualities, Epimetheus forgets to give light to mortals, being left with no qualities to attribute that will give them form. He does not have any more *dunameis* in the basket he is using for the distribution (*moira*). He confesses to his brother that he has committed a serious mistake [*faute*]: an oblivion. Prometheus goes to Olympia to make another mistake: to steal *technai* from Hephaestus and Athena to give to the mortals, in order to fill in [*suppléer*] their default of quality, but this also means that the destiny of the mortals is precisely to remain *prosthetic* and *without qualities*.

Mortals are beings without qualities, contrary to animals, to whom qualities were distributed: Plato describes how an equilibrium was progressively established between the species – to some velocity, to others strength, etc.

Since they have no qualities but those by default established prosthetically, so unlike animals, mortals are condemned to incessantly search for their fate, or, in other words, for their time. This temporality is founded on this fact: the *origin* of the mortals is a *default* of origin, therefore the mortals have no origin. Humans are in a certain way only *by default*; they are only what they become. But we will see how this myth claims that this default of origin can and should be raised to its *de jure* status: how this default can be necessary [*qu'il faille ce défaut*], how this default can become what is needed [*ce qu'il faut*] – what is needed *like the law*.

By being without qualities and by not agreeing about their ends, these failing beings go to war against one another until Zeus realises that they are threatening each other and are about to self-destruct. Thus Zeus asks Hermes to compensate the default of qualities by inscribing in their soul two feelings: *dikē* and *aidos*. *Dikē* is justice. *Aidos* is often translated as 'modesty' or 'shame' but also as 'honour', though undoubtedly it also means 'reserve' or 'restraint'; it is almost synonymous with *metron*, 'measure'. Nietzsche translated as 'shame' what I would instead call the feeling of finitude, the experience of mortality, or rather the experience of non-immortality, of radical fragility. This essential dwelling between the error and the fall [*la chute*] is what Heidegger calls 'facticity', but also the feeling of vanity, decay or decline (*Verfallen*).

Aidos would be a knowledge of the limits. I call this 'reserve' [*vergogne*].[6] The human is a being without limits, since he is a thief, an artificial being, a being of trickery, *mimēsis* and technics. For this reason, Zeus gives humans a feeling of limits, which can only be assigned positively, by itself – and not only as a feeling – by exercising *dikē* and *aidos*, without having assigned any rules to them in advance. The human can only assign himself his limits with the *interpretation* of the law. This interpretation, which is a juridical and ethical question, is not arbitrary, and it can never be given in advance. The law is neither a rule nor a regulation but above all a *question*, which should be *interpreted*.

Not only does Hermes bring to mortals the feelings of *dikē* and *aidos* but he is also the god of writing. The passion for *logos* that I spoke about earlier was born with writing, and eventually the question of *hermeneia*, interpretation, is at the heart of the philosophical question.

The question of interpretation is a question of time, and this myth shows that time is made of decisions and interpretations, thus beginning from an originary technicity or a prostheticity, that is, a default of origin. Human beings are guileful [*artificieux*] and technical since they do not find their being inside themselves but *in the milieu* composed of prostheses that they make and invent. This means that humans are free and destined to wander; this is what I called the originary disorientation. They have to *invent* their being-there, their existence. This is why Heidegger calls the 'to-be' (*Zu-sein*) the freedom or the responsibility of the self. But contrary to Heidegger's point of view, it is not alienated but *constituted* by technics, and made possible by technicity.

This mythological formulation finds an extraordinary scientific counterpart in André Leroi-Gourhan's *Gesture and Speech*, published in two volumes in 1964 and 1965.[7] This *magnum opus* is taken from the human prehistorical and palaeontological works that Leroi-Gourhan conducted after working for a long time in ethnography, especially in ethnography of technics mainly in the Pacific and in the Orient. It is from exploring these questions of ethnography of technics that he was led to study human fossils. Nowadays, he is mostly known as a prehistorian, and he worked particularly on the consequences of the discovery of what we called at that time Zinjanthropus, from 1959 in South Africa by Mary and Louis Leakey.

The Zinjanthropus is an Australopithecus, dated at 1.75 million years – and whose bipedal ascendants could go back to 3.6 million years. She weighs thirty kilos and is a real biped: she has an occipital hole exactly perpendicular to the tip of her skull. She has freed her anterior members of motivity, and they are now essentially devoted to making and expressing, or generally for externalisation. Her skeleton was found with her tools in the Olduvai Gorge. It is from these facts that Leroi-Gourhan shows what makes the human a rupture in the history of life: the apparition of a new type of living being. We call this progressive apparition a process of 'hominisation'. The humanity of humans is, for Leroi-Gourhan, a *process of technical externalisation of the living*. In other words, something that until now belonged to the living has moved outside the realm of the living, for instance, the conditions of predation and defence, like the struggle for life – although this last point is under-developed in Leroi-Gourhan; this is why I have emphasised this point in my work more strongly than him.[8] The human is a being who conducts his struggle for the life of non-biological organs, since technics is made of artificial organs.

Another argument that Leroi-Gourhan raises, and this is crucial, is that he shows that technics is a vector of memory. From the Australopithecus to the Neanderthal, we have moved from the split pebble that we make by hitting a pebble with another pebble to get a splinter, to the hundreds of types of objects from the Neanderthal times. While for the former tool we get a sharp spike in a few gestures (but a great technicity is already required to get a splinter), in the latter group of tools the most successful are true jewellery of flint, requiring hundreds of series of gestures that make up vast operational sequences and constituting a technicity of an extremely refined craftsmanship, from three hundred thousand years ago.

A biological differentiation is produced between the Australopithecus and the Neanderthals at the level of the cerebral cortex: this is what we call the opening of the cortical fan [*l'éventail cortical*]. But it is with the Neanderthal, Leroi-Gourhan argues, that the cortical system has almost stopped its evolution. This means that the neuronal equipment of the Neanderthal is quite similar to ours. Yet, even since the Neanderthal, technics has evolved immensely. This means that the technical evolution no longer depends on biological evolution.[9] The technical concept is not inscribed in advance in the biological brain. In this sense, we can argue that 'hominisation' is a process of externalisation: the space of differentiation is produced outside and independently of the strictly biological space, outside the 'interior milieu' in which, according to Claude Bernard, the constitutive elements of the organism are immersed.

Yet this process of externalisation is also the process of constitution
of what I call the third layer of memory. Since the neo-Darwinian
molecular biologists, and after the works of August Weismann at the
end of the nineteenth century, it is accepted that human sexual beings
are constituted of two memories: the memory of the species that we now
call the genome, and that Weismann called the *germen*, and the memory
of the individual, that is, the so-called somatic memory, preserved in
the central nervous system, which is also the memory of experience.
This exists from the great pond snails from Geneva's lake studied by
Piaget[10] all the way to chimpanzees, and, in between, insects and all the
vertebrates. It is for this reason that we can train [*dresser*] a dog, a hawk
or a cow: since there is a margin of indetermination in the individual
memory, there is neuronal plasticity that makes learning possible. But
in human beings, there is a third memory that animals do not have:
technics that both supports and constitutes this third memory. A sharpened flint is a form in an inorganic matter that is nevertheless organised
by sharpening it: the technical gesture 'engrams' an organisation that
transmits via the inorganic, opening for the first time in the history of life
the possibility to transmit knowledges that were individually acquired,
but by a way that is not biological. This is why technics is indissociable
from human memory: what makes this memory human is its spirituality
as well as the possibility to transmit from generation to generation. It is
this direct transmission of individual experiences between generations
that is forbidden in the animal kingdom, and this is why there is neither
an animal 'culture' nor an animal spirit – or, to put it more simply, there
is no heredity possible for acquired characters. But if you show me that
certain apes have such cultures, I include them in the human world. To
put it differently, given the first nascent factors of this third memory, I
undoubtedly let them enter into human history. This is also why they
give the impression of being so close to us.

Human memory is indissociable from technics as it is *epiphylogenetic*; I
use this term since this third type of memory is the product of both individual experience, which we call epigenetic, and a phylogenetic medium
[*support*], which constitutes a real intergenerational cultural phylum. This
accumulation of knowledges can no longer be called human species, but
rather humankind.

The knowledge of the slave in *Meno* begins in this primordial exteriority of memory to draw or trace a figure in the sand: to think his object,
right away he needs to externalise this object by organising the sand, by

organising the inorganicity of the sand, which then becomes the space and the medium of projection of the geometrical concept – the sand is here a plastic surface that can receive and, more importantly, retain an inscription. No matter how short-lived [*éphémère*] it is, the drawing on the sand can preserve a character of an element of the figure longer than the spirit of the slave, since the spirit of the slave is by essence changing [*mouvant*]: his thoughts do not cease to pass and to fade away; he is retentionally finite (and I will come back to this word 'retention'). In other words, his memory always fails [*flanche*], his attention is always diverted to new objects, and it is difficult for him to 'intentionalise', as Husserl would put it, the geometrical object –intentionalising means here to keep in sight [*le prendre en vue*] in his organic identity, in his necessity, in his intimate essence. Drawing is therefore indispensable to this potential philosopher (the slave), and the acting out of this potential, that is, his *anamnesis*. This drawing constitutes what I have called elsewhere a crutch of the understanding [*une béquille de l'entendement*], and a space of intuition that is entirely produced by the gestures of the slave who traces in the sand, throughout his reasoning, the figured effects of this reasoning, the sand preserving them as the results that the slave, together with his intuition and his understanding, has 'under sight' and upon which he can extend and *construct* geometrical reasoning.

Yet this is possible for the slave only because of his immersion in a language that guides him: it provides him with *terms* that he has previously conceived in his usage and his practice of language, for instance, 'line' or 'surface'. This linguistic immersion [*bain*] that precedes the slave's geometrical reasoning overdetermines the manner in which he traces and interprets the lines in the sand. Considering these lines, and before developing further this crucial point of the relation between language and the tracing that it overdetermines, we need to recall that, in a properly geometrical sense, the point does not exist – when we understand by *existing* something that stands in space and time. Although a point is not spatial, it is a *condition* of space. Indeed, we cannot say that a point is spatial, otherwise in this case it would already be a surface. As Euclid argues, a point is that which does not have any parts, and a line is a length without any width. Neither does the surface, in the geometrical sense, exist since it is a dimension without volume: it is an *ideality* constituted by other idealities, which are points and lines . . . that do not exist. A point is the possible intersection of two lines, a line is constituted of points, and a surface is constituted by the intersection of at least three lines; all these are idealities. Only with idealities is it possible to construct the geometrical figure. But this figure is only an image projection that is intuitive of ideal elements in real space. It constitutes in turn the possibility to think space, but these idealities are not themselves spatial, neither real nor existing as such [*existants*]. These concern the *apriority of experience*; they are a condition of experience (in existence). These constitute, as Kant would put it, the a priori elements of the pure form (without any content) of the *intuition* of space.

It is however required to figure the point in order to conceptualise it as a mathematical ideality, it is required to *intuitively* project it to project reasonings, and it is also in this sense that externalising is necessary to the figure: this figure is an image that allows the projection of what Kant calls a schema, what allows the unification of the understanding and intuition. The thought of space as this a priori form supposes this capacity of projection that represents the figure. What is crucial for us is to note that this projection is an externalisation: it allows a projection for intuition, but more importantly it constitutes a retentional space. This space is a medium of memory that supports progressively the reasoning of the temporal flow (what reason is when it thinks).

Husserl developed all of this at the end of his life in *The Origin of Geometry*, and in obvious contradiction to the entirety of his phenomenological oeuvre that preceded this late short text.[11] Husserl called the person who instituted geometry the 'protogeometer', the person who for the first time had the apodictic evidence of a geometric reasoning before his eyes, who had access for the first time to geometric ideality (we can think of Thales, poet and founder of a city-state, and the famous author of the theorem bearing his name). In discussing the memory of this protogeometer, he concludes that his memory is therefore finite – much like his life. And this bears two consequences:

1. To fix his reasoning on a figure, the geometer needs the power to fix it in the letter: *step by step*. Since the geometrical object is not exactly found in experience – it is a priori – it is constructed from the flow of thought. It should be considered as a flow of thought. But this flow is, as it implies, essentially changing [*mouvant*]: reasoning is a course, an unstable stream where thoughts are sequenced; it is an identity that these thoughts attempt to apprehend. What is sought by thinking is precisely the definition of the object's identity, that is, its stability, beyond the diversity of its successive appearances, occurring in the

stream of thought. The geometer thus needs both to draw and to write to be able to objectivise and to fix his own reasoning, to reconsider afterwards in critical distance, to interrupt it and to take it up again where he has left it and, as Leibniz puts it, 'to examine it at a leisurely pace'.

2. Yet writing is the technical condition but also the transcendental condition of possibility to constitute the *we* [*le nous*], it is reason as science: the 'subject' of geometry, which constitutes an infinite task, notes Husserl, is not an *I* [*un je*], but a transcendental *We* [*nous*]. This *We* is only possible according to the conditions of the epiphylogenetic media, as I called it earlier. In the case of geometry, all things are conditioned by ortho-graphic writing. *Geometry is de facto a dialogue between geometers* – beginning with the isolated geometer who can dialogue with himself through time; in this sense he can think *dia-lectically*, both *dia-chronically* and hermeneutically, giving a difference in the repetition. The old reasonings can be taken up again and confronted with current reasonings, to address messages to himself as it were, and to submit his own work to the principle of non-contradiction, by unifying the flow of successive thoughts.

The drawn figure and writing are two indispensable conditions of geometry, as the two dimensions of exteriority. There can not be geometry without the figure; its elements (point, line, surface, angle, hypotenuse, etc.) are defined by a language that raises them as idealities. But this language can posit them as *definitions* only if this language can record itself ortho-graphically. This allows one to engram the work of thinking step by step and to the letter, without losing any semantic substance.

There is a history of epiphylogenesis, and it is impossible to account for the possibility of knowledges without specifying the epiphylogenetic *stages* inside which these knowledges are produced. This epiphylogenetic immersion contains both language and technics, both the symbol and the tool: language and technics come from the same process of externalisation; they are, as Leroi-Gourhan puts it, two aspects of an absolutely new and unique reality in the history of life. But what it is essential to remember is that this externalisation does not precede any interiority, on the contrary, it immediately produces an *internalisation* – it is always at once and the same time *internalisation* and *externalisation*. Language is partly essentially related to the technical reality, when we understand it as a social product that is not constituted by a genetic determination, but by being a structure, it bears its own dynamic, making it a system. I inherit this system that I can internalise and modify – in the case of language, it is as a game of rules, and in the case of technics, it is as a functional organisation. I call these two faces of externalisation *techno-logics* [*la techno-logique*]. The moment of internalisation is often forgotten, which leads one to overlook the primordial exteriority, as the water that the fish can never see – since it can only see *inside* water. Thus Kant seems to believe that number 5, or number 1,000, are concepts that my mind [*esprit*] can have an a priori access to, by neglecting the fact that number 1,000 is strictly unconceivable without a system of written numeration, whose advent is very recent in the history of the human spirit.[12]

Plato puts these words in Socrates' mouth: the soul is immortal and has already contemplated the essences in an earlier life; the soul can therefore re-gain [*re-trouver*] essences. Hence the examples previously introduced: the calculation of the square by the slave, or the search for the knowledge of the essence of virtue by Meno. Plato already posits that there is some *already-there*, and that it is in this already-there that one finds both questions and solutions. But contrary to Plato, I think that this already-there is *essentially an outside* and that this outside, that is, the *world*, is submitted, in his organisation, to the epiphylogenetic condition that modifies, throughout its evolutions, the life of the inside. Regarding this 'inside', it internalises the outside, but in internalising it, it forgets it: it forgets its own operation and thus naturalises its own knowledge. For instance, numeration, which is first and foremost a motor and corporal system: a set of gestures that have been learned at length (to use fingers to count, then abacuses[13] or multiplying tables, and finally the mind) and that have later become embodied under the form of a mental calculation, *in forgetting that it all began with the hands.*

Kant's mistake was to believe that this 'mentality' (its mental character) of calculation precedes the possibility to calculate manually, 'digitally'. Consciousness needs *de facto* what Kant calls a schema: this takes an a priori form; it is a form that the stream of *all* consciousness *necessarily* takes, *to be able to* conceive a number. But the realised conception of this number is supposed by its *externalisation* and, simultaneously, its internalisation under the form of a numeration system. In other words, an external image supports the production of the schema, which is in turn supposed by motor behaviours, gestures. Kant's mistake continues to be made by cognitivism, for instance with the theory of 'mentalese', proposed by Jerry Fodor, who draws from Noam Chomsky, where it is argued in short that there is a 'language of thought' that is pre-inscribed in the brain. What is neglected as much by classical metaphysics as by contemporary cognitive metaphysics is the question that we will now turn to, that of *tertiary retention.* I have created this concept in a contradictory dialogue with the phenomenology of time.

Notes

1. [Trans.] Stiegler uses *thèse* to mean both a thesis (as in 'position' in philosophy) and also a doctoral dissertation, referring to the physical scholarly work.

2. [Trans.] Stiegler's main argument regarding Plato makes use of the chronological order of Plato's work. *Meno* is considered by Plato specialists as an early work, written before *Phaedrus*, in which a certain type of writing as *pharmakon* is denounced. Stiegler follows Derrida's famous analysis of Plato's *Phaedrus* in Jacques Derrida, 'Plato's Pharmacy', in *Dissemination*, trans. Barbara Johnson (London: Continuum, 2004), pp. 67–186.

3. [Trans.] Cybernetics comes from the Greek *kyvernitiki*, meaning 'government', and *kyverno* also means 'to steer', 'to pilot' or 'to govern'.

4. [Trans.] The quotation marks here denote the deliberate ambiguity that Stiegler adds to the text. In French, *explication* means not only 'explanation' or 'analysis' but also 'argument' or 'fight'.

5. Plato, *Protagoras*, trans. C. C. W. Taylor (Oxford: Oxford University Press, 2002), 320d, p. 13.

6. On this specific point, see *Symbolic Misery, Vol. 1: The Hyperindustrial Epoch*, trans. Daniel Ross (Cambridge: Polity Press, 2014), pp. 11–12, and *Technics and Time, Vol. 4: Symbols and Diabols, or the War of Spirits*, forthcoming.

7. [Trans.] These two volumes were translated into English as a single book: André Leroi-Gourhan, *Gesture and Speech*, trans. Anna Bostock Berger (Cambridge, MA: MIT Press, 1993).

8. See *Technics and Time, Vol. 1: The Fault of Epimetheus*, trans. Richard Beardsworth and George Collins (Stanford: Stanford University Press, 1998), chapter 2, pp. 82–133.

9. [Trans.] This leads Stiegler to develop a post-Darwinian position, referring to 'technical selection' as a transformation and a supplement of Darwin's theory of natural and artificial selection. Stiegler defended this position in his 2013 seminars at École d'Épineuil-le-

Fleuriel (see <pharmakon.fr>), in reading Charles Darwin's *The Descent of Man* (1871). See Gerald Moore, 'On the Origin of *Aisthesis* by Means of Artificial Selection, or the Preservation of Favoured Traces in the Struggle for Existence', *boundary 2*, 44.1 (2017).

10. Jean Piaget, 'Les Limnées des lacs de Neuchâtel, Bienne, Morat et des environs', *Conchyliologie*, 5 (1912), pp. 311–22, and 'L'Adaptation de la *Limnaea stagnalis* aux milieux lacustres de la Suisse romande. Étude biometrique et génétique', *Revue Suisse de Zoologie*, 36.17 (1929), pp. 1–268.

11. Edmund Husserl, 'The Origin of Geometry', in Jacques Derrida, *Edmund Husserl's Origin of Geometry: An Introduction*, trans. John P. Leavey Jr (Lincoln, NE: University of Nebraska Press, 1989), pp. 157–80. This obvious contradiction at first surprised the young Jacques Derrida until he made it the first argument of his own philosophy.

12. On this particular topic, the question of schematism in Kant, see *Technics and Time, Vol. 3: Cinematic Time and the Question of Malaise*, trans. Stephen Barker (Stanford: Stanford University Press, 2011), pp. 49–54.

13. 'Apart from the most primitive languages, all languages know a system of numeral words to designate prime numbers (in general until 9) and superior units (in general a few powers of 10); with them we make names for other numbers by procedures that need to reflect addition and multiplication. Let us note however that at times we encounter the formation of numerals of subtractive principles; thus in Latin: *duo-deviginti*, two of twenty, for 18. These systems of formation of numeral names are limited by the restrained number of names of superior units. On the contrary, the representation of natural numbers on an abacus is more algorithmic and is limited; numbers are given according to tokens following a positional principle: the value of a token is determined by the row where it is placed. A small number is given by the corresponding number of tokens in the first row; in the next row (on the left), the value of a token equals the next unit of the system (for instance 10), and so on. Often we find intermediary units (5 in between 1 and 10, 50 in between 10 and 100, and so on). Most numeral notation systems were a compromise between the linguistic system and that of the abacus.' Hans Freudenthal, 'Notation mathématique', *Encyclopædia Universalis*, 1972.

3. Consciousness in the Age of Industrial Temporal Objects

ÉD: In this vertiginous journey that led us from the myth of Epimetheus, as told by Protagoras and Plato, to the Neanderthal, without forgetting the Australopithecus, we witness the birth of mnemotechnics. It is a real anthropogenesis: the making of the human through the technics of memory.

BS: One needs to carefully distinguish between technics as a milieu of the epiphylogenetic memory in general, and mnemotechnics. By being a technical being, the human is also a cultural being: this third technical memory that surrounds him has allowed him to accumulate an intergenerational experience that we often call 'culture'. This is why it is absurd to oppose technics and culture: technics is the condition of culture that permits its transmission. However, *our* time is the era of technics, we can call it *technology*: it is defined by the crisis of culture, due to its industrialisation and its submission to the imperatives of market efficiency. We will come back to this point later on.

While technics in general constitutes for the human an originary milieu of epiphylogenetic memory, any given technics is not however *made to* retain memory. A sharpened flint is not meant to retain memory. It is made to slice the meat and work on matter. It happens to also be, spontaneously, a vector of memory. This is why archaeologists can, through a sharpened flint, or through the shards of pottery, through any given manufactured objects, reconstitute a civilisation. Gestures are preserved in objects that are all, some more evidently than others, the media of recordings. They record the human motor function but are also recordings of human behaviour, and particularly the human spirit.

It is from this general epiphylogenetics that, around thirty or forty thousand years ago but perhaps ever since the Neanderthal and the first funeral practices, mnemotechnic usages arrived. With no hesitation I include the mnemotechnics found in cave art. By then, human groupings start developing technics and behaviours made to transmit memory; amongst them, we can include the *Churinga* (or *Tjurunga*) and all other forms of mythograms and inscriptions [*engrammages*], for instance, the Amerindian cords made of knots and tattoos inscribed on sorcerers' bodies, which are also instruments used to calculate.

But it is after the Neolithic age, a little over ten thousand years ago and around the time of sedentary settlement, that entire systems of numeration develop. These will give birth to what are now known as systems of writing. The sedentariness that led to urban civilisation happened in a region that is today in Iraq, and where the Mesopotamian empire would soon appear. It is the passage from the hunter-gatherer to the farmer and the cultivator, who already produces a primitive form of capital accumulation, that is, an excess in comparison to his immediate needs. This will allow 'investments', accomplishments in technical, artistic, religious and sumptuary domains but also in utilities, for instance, the networks of irrigation and pyramids that correspond to what we often more commonly refer to as signs of civilisation.

Agriculture thus allows the accumulation of stock listed in accounting books – hence we encounter around that time the first accounting systems, which consist in inscriptions on diverse media together with calculations from these inscriptions. Rapidly, these systems of numeration would allow the production of calendar systems (they appear in Mesopotamia around the fourth millennium BC, and in Egypt this system already denotes 365 days in the third millennium). These bring to collective life a capacity to anticipate weather variations associated with seasons and, particularly, rises in the water level (the Tigris, the Euphrates and the Nile). In this way, in the era of great empires, the combination of two facts produces new potentialities: the alluvial wealth of the great lakes together with the technics of written notation makes it possible to anticipate rises in water levels and therefore to produce the optimal exploitation of the soils' alluvial fertility. The systems of notation would progressively improve from this period onwards. During the space of two thousand years, mnemotechnics would transform from hieroglyphs to modern alphabets.

The alphabetic writing that we continue to use (even on computer keyboards) appears with the Greeks, and this alphabetisation constitutes, strictly speaking, the Greek city-state: it is its condition of possibility. The Greek city-state is a community that lives in the *critical* knowledge of its rules of life. Due to their public nature, they are known, described and criticisable; these rules of life are the law. The city-state can only have such a critical knowledge of these rules of life because these are external-ised and objectivised in the form of a written text and can be discerned in a flow of speech. This flow is in turn discretised by writing and the entire community can have critical access to this text since the technics used is alphabetical: a system of diacritical signs that is economical and made of fewer than thirty characters that each person can learn to use both as a reader and as a scribe. This way, the Greek city-state is the first community where schools emerge.

But, on the other hand, the alphabet brings the possibility to access once again in a literal way – in other words, in a quasi-exact manner – what happens in thought, the *passage* and the *past* of what a thought is. If one were to read *Meno*, for instance, one has direct access to Plato's thought, regardless of what Plato himself can say about *hypomnesis*. You can interpret this text in a variety of ways, in the same way that you would interpret Plato's speech in his presence. You could make the same objection that Plato himself makes in *Phaedrus*: that Plato could defend his own interpretation of his own speech [*parole*]. But who can claim that Plato is the best interpreter of his own speech? Besides, he can himself change the interpretation of his own speech in time. I believe that this is exactly what happened in the case of Plato. I do not think that Plato interprets the myth of Persephone at the time of *Meno* in the same way that he would interpret it at the time of *Phaedrus* or *Republic*. All of us interpret differently throughout our life; fortunately, we change our point of view on the world and on ourselves. This means that we do not understand our own speech and words in the same way as times change; this also means that our words [*paroles*] are essentially open to an indefinite number of possible interpretations that are all testifying to the openness of the future, as many chances as time brings us. But this does not mean, of course, that all interpretations are equal. Everybody knows that while Richter and Gould give very different interpretations of Bach, and are very remarkable, all interpretations of Bach are not equal.

When you read the sentences from Plato's *Meno*, you do not feel that you only have an approximate image of what Plato thought: you are in an *immediate* relation to Plato's thought, and you know it intimately. You are in the very *element* of Plato's thought.

Yet the situation is rather different when dealing with cuneiform statements. The reading of the cuneiform statements of Mesopotamians continues to be irreducibly associated with a relative uncertainty concerning the meanings [*sens*] of those statements. There can be no doubt as to the sense of the written statements by Plato and the sense of the discussion. Meaning is not the same thing as signification – 'meaning is use', as Wittgenstein puts it.[1] The tone and the prosody are not preserved in the orthographic literal recording, hence the invention of the phonograph.

The alphabet is the appearance of the first mnemotechnics that uses a strictly 'orthothetic' character.[2] I had to create this neologism from the Greek *orthotēs* and *thesis*. *Orthotēs* means 'exactitude', and *thesis* 'position'. What I call an 'orthothetic statement' (for instance, alphabetic statements) posits exactly the past. This way, it allows for an intensification of the cumulation, which I was referring to earlier in relation to technics in general and to mnemotechnics in particular. It constitutes in itself a sudden accumulation of innumerable traces (that would be gathered in the library of Alexandria before it burned down). Here a cumulation reaches an obvious qualitative threshold since Plato not only writes, which is essential to his own manner of philosophising (regardless of the vices of *hypomnesis*), but what he writes becomes readable *to the letter*; it becomes possible to continue the dialogue with him in his absence. This is precisely what Aristotle ends up doing, but also the neoplatonists, and what eventually all philosophy would do – this is what I do at this very moment when talking with you about Plato and dia-loguing with you *through* Plato, citing some of his works, from which I could – if we had time – cite to the letter to comment word by word.

Yet this possibility of commentary is also that of *anamnesis*: contrary to what Plato believes, *anamnesis* is far from being the contrary of *hypomnesis*; rather, the latter conditions the former. But this is an ambiguous condition, as we will see; *hypomnesis* can always prevent *anamnesis*, as Plato had feared. My dispute with Plato is not when he affirms that *hypomnesis* constitutes a danger – and I will soon show to what extent we live today in a dangerously hypomnesic era. My disagreement lies in the Platonic argument that *anamnesis* is the opposite of *hypomnesis*. I believe, contrary to Plato, that in fact *anamnesis is the good way of practising hypomnesis*. But this also means – and I will come back to this in *Symbols and Diabols* – that we need to overcome dialectics as such when it calls for a principle of contradiction, since hypomnesic textuality is structurally open to a multiplicity of interpretations: such is the dia-chronicity of thought.

What allows me to dialogue with Plato today (and what made it possible for Plato to engage in a dialogue with himself, throughout the lifetime of his thought) is the written form Plato has given to his thought. And by having this written form, I can *re-actualise* this thought, or, as Husserl put it, I can *reactivate* it with a new intuition. It is this possibility of reactivation, locked in the *literality* of Greek texts, that always includes an analytical and a critical moment. Thus it always constitutes a polemical moment conferred in the original point as a kind of ray of light that gives us a clear and distinct vision of Greece that continues to impose itself on us even today. We feel that light started shining all of a sudden in Greece, what we call the Greek miracle. There is also, of course, the erection of the Parthenon, but this is closely linked to writing itself. This 'light' is in fact the effect of an era of epiphylogenesis. Far from being a pure and simple enlightenment [*illuminisme*], its support is really material.

On the back of the human's epiphylogenetic situation, mnemotechnics also appeared tens of thousands of years ago, and became scripts from the Neolithic period, in which the alphabet plays a fundamental role around the seventh century BC; it coincides with the emergence of the West [*Occident*], and far from Greece, the first books of the Bible are being written, from the eleventh century BC onwards, in a form consonant with the alphabet.

Mnemotechnics allows the material retention of time, the preservation of the past in a reactivable form, using the characteristics intrinsic to each mnemotechnics. I argue that the study of the conditions of functioning of the individual and collective consciousness is fundamentally conditioned by the study of technics, which in turn gives consciousness access into its own past. This is obviously a particularly significant question today, when mnemotechnics has become mnemotechnologies: the very heart of industrial development.

What I called consciousness's 'own past' is not only the past that was lived by this consciousness. I, Bernard Stiegler, am not only what I have lived since my birth fifty-one years ago: I am also, in a way, all this past that I have been referring to from the beginning of these interviews, that lives in me, haunts me, possesses me as a spirit and what these spirits give to a place, and make it their place by opening a time where something happens. Everything that I have been talking about since the beginning of these interviews, Plato, the Egyptians, Mesopotamia, the Neanderthals and the Australopithecus, one way or another, I *am* all of this, or at least I inherit all of this, which in turn constitutes me in an essential manner. All this past, I have re-actualised it through the accumulated traces that I have inherited in the form of 'culture' (combined with my genetic inheritance, which obviously also has its own role to play). My past is only *mine*, but it is also the past that I was transmitted in the form of knowledge. This is the epiphylogenetic stratum, and in particular the mnemotechnic stratum, what I called earlier the three forms of memory of living humans, that makes the transmission of knowledge possible.

In this sense, I believe, contrary to Plato, that technics is constitutive of human knowledge. This does not mean that human knowledge should be reduced to what is retained by the material retentions: human knowledge is also, and in an essential way, human *desire*. These material retentions give rise to an inheritance because they are fetishised, and charged with phantasms and affects. What makes the human a knowledgeable being is that he is desiring, with phantasms and imaginations: he is only a knowledgeable being on the condition of *being passionate about knowledge*, and properly hallucinated by the apparitions of the geometrical figures, for instance. This is what Diotima argues in Plato's *Symposium*. Knowledge is what does not leave indifferent, and in this sense it affects: it is what is not insipid, but on the contrary it is *the sapid par excellence*. It is what manifests itself as salience – what becomes evident: significance as such, which literally means that which signals [*ce qui fait signe(s)*]. More generally, knowledge manifests itself first and primordially as beauty: knowledge is first what is beautiful (for the person who knows). This is why, in the beautiful *Symposium*, knowledge takes place in the figure of Eros: there, desire is the *condition* of knowledge. However, we know since Freud that the condition of *desire* is the fetish as prosthesis – although I think Freud has never really seriously thought about the technicity or the prostheticity of desire, or of humanity as a whole, in spite of everything that he wrote about the 'prosthetic God' that the human has 'become' in *Civilization and its Discontents*.[3]

Yet knowledge as sapidity seems to be threatened by liquidation. This is what also anticipates Hegel (without knowing it as it were) when he argues that it is high time for philosophy to 'lay aside the title of "*love* of knowing" and be *actual* knowing'.[4] How have this 'laying aside' of the name of love for philosophy and the resulting liquidation of the sapidity of knowledge become possible?

This concerns a hypomnesic mutation, that knowledge has not yet managed to give it a sapidity, and this illustrates the justness of the Platonic prevention against *anamnesis*, resulting from a metaphysical position. This opposition between *anamnesis* and *hypomnesis* should be overcome.

The alphabetical script is a literal synthesis of memory. From the nineteenth century, with the Industrial Revolution, new technics of preservation of memory would appear, new orthotic mnemotechnics, comparable to the literal synthesis but in a new sense. There were technologies of analogic synthesis of visual and auditory perception: photography and phonography, much like the alphabet, can preserve and transmit in an exact way by fixing an element of the past or a perception on to a material medium. But this no longer concerns the meaning of an oral statement, whose orthographic symbols reconstruct the diacriticity of the phonemes of language and, through them, the meaning of, let's say, the luminous and sonorous frequencies produced by an object of perception – the voice of an opera singer or a tragic actor, the sound of an orchestra, the luminous frequencies emitted by a landscape or a face.

In this moment, we are recording a radio show ahead of its broadcast [*en temps différé*]. I speak to you in this microphone and through it an analogic and orthothetic sonorous image of my voice comes to rest on the magnetic film of the tape recorder, in the form of a slight modification of the electromagnetic state of this medium, which will keep it in the form of a trace [*empreinte*] whose variations correspond analogically to the variations of the frequencies of the streaming of my voice. If we look at this signal on the oscilloscope, we can see a graphic representation of time/frequency that is an analogue to the variations of the sound of my voice. The radio listeners will hear my voice in a few days through their radio receivers and they will not think that they are hearing an image of my voice. Since this radio programme is not a live broadcast [*un faux direct*], they might even believe that I am speaking at the exact moment that they are listening to me. The radio listeners will be sure, and rightly so, that they are hearing my voice itself and not the image of my voice. This is the effect produced by the orthothetic character of a recording, whether it is literal or analogic: in the same way that I am certain of having direct access to Plato's own thought when I read a book of his, if I were to listen to a recording of the voice of Sarah Bernhardt, the emotion comes from my certitude at hearing not an image of what Sarah Bernhardt's voice could have been, but her voice itself, and therefore Sarah Bernhardt herself – even though she is dead and buried.

From the nineteenth century, new orthotheses are therefore capable of reconstituting strata of the past that are larger than the stock [*fonds*] of the book-based civilisation – in which sculpture, painting and other artistic forms representing the past co-existed, but were not exactly orthothetic recordings. To sum up what we have discussed so far, we can say that the human is a epiphylogenetic being and that in the history of epiphylogenesis, which began two million years ago as a process of externalisation, probably around tens of thousands of years ago appeared mnemotechnics, and then with the Neolithic, systems of written notation that gave rise to the first orthothetic synthesis (the alphabet). We need to add to this brief history the analogic orthothetic synthesis that happened in the nineteenth century first with photography, then phonography, and then in the twentieth century with cinematography, radio broadcasting and television.

The significance of the printing press as a technique of reproduction [*duplication*] needs to be explained. This mechanical technics of reproduction only amplified the effect of the literal synthesis and did not constitute in itself a new form of synthesis. It should be considered as a development of the alphabetic orthothesis that expands its effects much further, but it does not constitute a new orthothetic synthesis in itself. However, this opened a new era of epiphylogenesis.

In the second half of the twentieth century, the digital orthothetic synthesis appeared, first with computers [*l'informatique*], and now, at the beginning of this twenty-first century, in the form of electronic appliances of all sorts, such as video cameras, cameras, mobile phones, but also voice recorders that are no longer analogic.

This is a new revolution of recording that is about to transform once again, and with considerable consequences, what I call with philosophy the '*ecstasy of temporality*' – in other words, the relations between the past, the future and the present.[5] The main consequences of the evolution of the epiphylogenetic stock (that constitutes humanity) are always the modifications of the relations between the three terms of the ecstasy of time. To put it differently, ever since the Industrial Revolution, and the development of new mnemotechnologies that contributed in large part to this revolution, especially in the nineteenth and twentieth centuries, we have kept on living disruptions in the conditions of temporisation, and therefore individuation. Individuation should be understood as a *process* by which we, as individuals or collectives, *become* who we *are*. We are in fact by essence temporal beings, and the epiphylogenetic media of our temporality condition in a primordial manner our relation to time. In other words, we are always to come, inasmuch as we continue to have a future and we are by essence in the future tense; we devote the totality of our energy and our care [*souci*] to anticipating (or at least in trying to do so, most of the time in vain, but not without any consequences) what we will become, and even what the world will become after our lives.

Yet I need to emphasise another point: since the epiphylogenetic becoming is now under the control of industries – the last two centuries were characterised by a process of industrialisation of memory – we are now in what I call an ecology of spirit, that is, a political and industrial economy that rests on the industrial exploitation of the specific times belonging to consciousness. Through this exploitation, masses of ego are formed as bodies of consumers; large global markets are constituted to absorb the ever larger investments made by large industries. In this situation, consciousnesses are degraded, since they are exploited at the limits of their temporal possibilities, in the same way that some territories or animal species are degraded or damaged.

To discern what is happening, the Husserlian theory of the temporal object is useful: cinematographic or phonographic recordings, which are now mostly broadcast by broadcasting industries, radio stations and TV channels, make audiovisual temporal objects. Unlike an ordinary physical object, a temporal object is constituted by its flow [*écoulement*]: the condition of its appearance and disappearance to my consciousness; it disappears as soon as it appears. For instance, the radio listeners who are listening to this show on France Culture can only hear me by letting my voice disappear. They cannot stop at what I just said, contrary to when they read a book. My radiographically transmitted words are structurally temporal: they are flowing. A melody is also a flow: a melody is a musical object precisely because this object is flowing.[6] Music is a composition of time and time is by essence what happens. Husserl has studied temporal objects since they present the specificity of being constituted by this structure of flow that is perfectly homogeneous to the flowing of my own consciousness: to know their fundamental structures is to learn something about the temporal structure of consciousness itself. Our consciousnesses are flowing, in this sense, they have a duration: this is the immediate data that Bergson refers to.[7] My consciousness is essentially duration and, therefore, a flow. At this very moment when I am speaking to you in this microphone, I am listening to myself, and together with me, my words testify that I am also flowing, these words are a radiographic realisation, but those who are listening are also flowing.

Yet, interestingly, there are objects that have themselves a flowing structure. The flowing of these objects, when I am conscious of the process, coincides entirely, or as Husserl puts it 'point by point', with the flowing of my own consciousness. This led Husserl to argue that, if I were to study these temporal objects and could therefore understand their internal structure, I would learn something of the internal structure of consciousness itself.

In his study of the temporal object, Husserl discovers the concept of primary retention. Suppose that you are listening to a melody. A melody is a succession of notes that have tonality levels and durations. This *succession* of notes is not only a succession of notes and sounds, since notes are only constituted by their succession and therefore by creating *relations* between these notes. To put it differently, these notes do not only succeed one another, they constitute preservations [*maintenances*] in the flow, but also recurrences and so on, using relations between tonality levels (intervals) and relations of durations (rhythms). A given note A, if you consider it independently and outside a musical context, is no longer the note A: it is a sonorous frequency today placed by the tuning fork at 440 hertz (this value was established by convention, at the international congress that met in London in 1939). It is the relation (or relations) that a given note A has with other sonorous frequencies that makes it the note A. It is with these other frequencies that it produces a stability that we call an interval, but that we also call, at the time of Pythagoras, a *logos*, a relation.

Husserl thinks the melody and the temporal object in general (a film is for instance such an object), which is *present* to my ear at the moment, *now*, when I listen to it. He argues that the specificity of this temporal object comes from *the presence* of the immediately preceding element. The temporal object starts from this presence. For instance, the note A retains a B flat that precedes it, which in turn retained another note that preceded it, let's say a C sharp, the whole constituting an arpeggio. But this unity of relations between these elements will constitute the melodicity as such – by forming a flow in continuity, a flowing that is the time of music. These relations certainly become more and more complex and rich as they contain 'preservations' that are also harmonic and polyphonic . . .

The note can only be constituted as a note by retaining in itself the previous note, thus the present of the temporal object is inhabited by an originary past, which Husserl names the 'just-having-been', *in the very perception* of the temporal object: it is the retaining of the present note that Husserl calls a *primary retention*. We can even show – as I did at length in *Cinematic Time and the Question of Malaise* – that the same thing happens in cinema; this is what Xavier Lemarchand called the Kuleshov Effect.[8] One day, the Russian stage director would have experimented[9] by editing [*monter*] a shot with the actor Ivan Ilyich Mozzhukhin, who was performing an undetermined and undecidable expression, maybe comparable to that of Da Vinci's famous Mona Lisa. Yet this same shot was edited with three different shots (a table of victuals, a corpse, a child), and what the spectators saw in each montage created three different expressions of Mozzhukhin, even though it was each time the same shot. This experience demonstrates once again that, much like the case of the music note in the melody, the symbolic and temporal power of the shot is realised by its capacity to retain primarily in itself the immediate recollection of the preceding shot. But this power is also extended in its capacity to 'protain' a scene to come, if I can put it this way, adapting Husserl's own concept of protention. In other words, the editing and the relations that are woven create an expectation of the following shot. This is what will make the unity of the sequence, sometimes in the form of a surprise, as a diversion or reversal of this expectation.[10]

Husserl teaches us that we need to distinguish between *primary* retention, which he discovered in the present of *perception*, and *secondary* retention, which constitutes the past and belongs to *imagination*. Secondary retention, which we usually call 'memory' [*souvenir*], belongs to the past while primary retention belongs to the present. Yet Husserl argued that there is *no relation* between primary and secondary retentions. This position, which seemed to me paradoxical (and which he does not maintain later on), is taken in the context of a debate that he had with Franz Brentano (in his lectures 'On the Phenomenology of the Consciousness of Internal Time'). Brentano taught and initiated Husserl to the study of the sound perception, leading Husserl to work on the question of temporal objects. Husserl argued that Brentano confused primary and secondary retentions, and therefore criticised his teacher for not understanding primary retention. For Brentano, primary retention is produced by the attribution of an indication of the past in the music note that precedes the current music note that I hear at this moment, and to him this indication is conferred by imagination. Husserl disagreed and argued that if this indication were produced by imagination, time would therefore be a product of imagination, and not the object of perception, and ultimately this argument would posit that time would not exist: it would only be an *illusion* of imagination, a *fiction*. Yet Husserl's starting point is, on the contrary, that the temporality of consciousness is what is most indubitable and most immediately subject to experimental research, similar to Bergson, for whom duration is an immediate data of consciousness. The point of view of Brentano is therefore unacceptable, and the indication of a past-being in primary retention is a product of perception. Hence we need to refer to primary retention, and to meticulously distinguish it from secondary retention, which derives from imagination.

Unfortunately, even though Husserl is entirely right against Brentano, his reasoning nonetheless led him to radically oppose primary and secondary retentions. He went so far as to claim that they have no relation, and in particular that primary retention does not owe anything to secondary retention. However, these two modes of retention are not opposed; on the contrary, they continuously compose. When I listen to the same melody twice in a row on two different days, and a fortiori when I listen to it ten times in a row (as has become common practice after phonographic recording), what happens differs since the more I listen to the melody, the more I would find differences in every listening of the melody: different *phenomena* are each time produced by the same *object*. The object is the melody and each time it is the same object. But each time a different phenomenon is produced, and if the music is good, I would hear new things each time, even though I have the impression of listening to the same object. Where does this difference between these *repetitions of the same* come from?

First, such a difference can only mean that primary retentions produced by my consciousness throughout the flowing of the temporal flux, which is also the flowing of my own time of consciousness, will change with each listening. My consciousness is therefore *active* in the listening of a melody: it *selects* among all possible primary retentions, and does not retain everything. This also explains why if we were to ask ten individuals – which I often do when I give my classes – to sum up the meaning of my speech from the last twenty minutes, these ten individuals would give ten different meanings. They would not be wrong, nor would I be right to suggest only one meaning to my own speech. This would simply demonstrate that each of us has selected primarily a type of retention, but above all that the difference between our primary retentions is closely linked to our secondary retentions, which are knowledge that we already had before listening to the statement. Here, what I call 'knowledge' is those secondary retentions accumulated by our past experiences and which constitute *as many horizons of expectations*, also called *protentions*.

Yet the role of secondary retentions as selection criteria in the primary retentions, and therefore as a horizon of expectation overdetermining the construction of a musical phenomenon during the listening of a musical temporal object, only becomes obvious with the arrival of the phonograph. This is what led me to introduce a third concept, formalised as a way to continue and critique Husserl's analyses: the concept of *tertiary retention*.

Something new and previously unconceivable happens with the phonograph: with this apparatus, the same temporal object, that is, the same interpretation of the same music piece, can be produced in the exact same way twice in a row. This makes possible the analogic and orthothetic synthesis of the audible. Before this invention, this synthesis was strictly impossible: an orchestra could play the same piece twice, but the two performances necessarily differ. The phonograph allowed one for the first time to repeat a temporal object – and obliged one to consider that when the same object is produced many times, different phenomena are produced every time.

I demonstrated in *Disorientation* that the literal and orthothetic synthesis of the voice has also made comparisons possible for the first time, but on a different plane. Hence the spatialisation of speech sound in the alphabetically written form has also permitted repetitions leading to an entirely original difference: the varied interpretation of written statements made by the same reader in different circumstances. This is what Foucault comments on with Seneca in 'Writing of the Self'.[11] The textual identification of a linguistic statement is *what gives the hermeneutic difference, strictly speaking*. What I call 'literal *différant* identification' is this literal tertiary retention that gives different and new readings in each repetition of the same text. The literal *différant* identification is the first case of an orthothetic tertiary retention.[12]

The phonogram is also a tertiary retention. Some tertiary retentions are orthothetic by nature but others are not. Examples of orthothetic tertiary retentions are phonogramic, photographic, cinematographic, alphabetic and diasthematic (as the notations on musical scores are called), and there are many other kinds. In fact, all the epiphylogenetic instances are tertiary retentions, that is, all objects in general, since all objects are technical objects. But all technical objects, as tertiary retentions, do not have the same characteristics.

The *properly mnemotechnic* tertiary retentions, which Plato would call hypomnesic, have controllable effects, and when these mnemotechnics are orthothetic, they open the era of history, law, philosophy, science and, finally, what we call the West [*Occident*], but the monotheism of the Islamic East [*Orient*] is also a historical concretisation very close to the West. Monotheism makes the era of culture a reality, and comes from the orthothetic literal retention.[13] And, in this respect, I often think of Islam, as with North America, as a non-European dimension of the West.

Moreover, my thesis is that the analogic and digital orthotheses open another era, and my hypothesis is that this era is probably the end of the West. It is at the same time a process of industrialisation and, therefore, of commodification of memory in all its forms (including biological, since genetic manipulations are 'tertiarisations' of the living); it is the theatre of a major crisis and perhaps catastrophic in the history of the spirit, as the general process deploying human, individual and collective temporality. This temporality is constituted by 'revenances' and repetitions that make the human epiphylogenetic situation possible. This situation leads to all sorts of global ill-beings, coinciding with the liquidation of the millennial processes of psychic and collective individuation, including the West and its different elements in particular. A multitude of extremely reactionary temptations are emerging, such as xenophobia, diverse fanaticisms (*laïcité* is one of them) and all possible forms of *ressentiment*. This is why our present is so worrying.

The epiphylogenetic recordings of the past, and in particular when they are orthothetic, overdetermine the relations that I make between primary and secondary retentions. This explains why, in the twentieth century, industries seized tertiary retentions to make what we call after Adorno cultural industries. With cinema, music, radio and television, and the broadcasting of audiovisual temporal objects, industries can perhaps not control but at least condition these times of consciousness and, for instance, make people adopt new behaviours. When these audiovisual temporal objects are flowing, they coincide with the time of the consciousnesses they are targeting, and these consciousnesses now form masses of consciousnesses, also called audience figures. These new behaviours encourage the consumption of products that large industries place in global markets. For instance, today, everyone might associate a given melody with a certain brand of tights or chewing gum, but certain images are also associated with this melody and this product

– for example, the brand of coffee for the family breakfast that Odile, played by Sabine Azéma, recalls when talking to Nicolas, played by Jean-Pierre Bacri, in Alain Resnais's *Same Old Song* [*On connaît la chanson*]. Nicolas shows Odile a family picture:

Odile – What does this picture remind me of? Ah yes! The advertisement for chicory, of course! You know what I mean?
Nicolas – The advertisement for chicory? No . . . I don't know it . . .
Odile – This family, you know, who's having breakfast in a corn field?
Nicolas – Ah yes, it rings a bell, yes . . .

The society of industrial temporal objects transforms our existence in prefabricated serials full of clichés, which we accumulate without paying much attention. The coincidence of the flowing time of industrial temporal objects together with the time of consciousnesses has the consequence that we adopt this time by making our own objects of consciousness (or attention). We adhere to them with such privacy that they become substitutes for the temporalities belonging to our own consciousnesses. This is the catastrophic use, by the cultural industries, of the virtues of temporal objects: this also leads to an ecological catastrophe in the epiphylogenesis as a mind/spirit milieu.

The ruin of this milieu is created when industries impose their criteria in an exclusive or hegemonic manner on the retentional phenomenon that characterises consciousness. We see the multiplication everywhere of delirious behaviours. These are the acting out of the worst phantasms found in all levels of society, everywhere on earth.

ÉD: Once we understand the role played by each of these retentions – primary, secondary, tertiary – and the way in which they intervene concretely in the constitution and the reception of the temporal objects, we are left wondering how this schema can make us think of a global phenomenon that seems at first sight to exceed the limits of the operating of consciousness. More specifically, I think of the industry of cultural objects that is increasingly an industry of temporal objects. Your last volume of Technics and Time *is called* Cinematic Time: *it is not entirely a work on cinema, even though it also refers to cinema. You use the concept of cinema, or rather the cinematic apparatus, as a paradigm to think of the functioning of consciousness as a production and editing of time. This paradigm supports a strong thesis: the hyperindustrial production – which goes beyond industrial production – of temporal objects that we witness comes with a general synchronisation of consciousnesses.*

BS: Yes, I believe that such a process is taking place: a process of generalisation of industrial production of temporal objects leads to the tendency of generalised synchronisation. There are obviously some counter-tendencies, but unfortunately they seem to be weaker than the dominant tendency. I have to admit that this perspective described in *Cinematic Time* is infernal, and I envisaged the end of the title, 'The Question of Malaise', as a warning. I try to show that today's society is suffering, leading to a situation in which the tendency towards generalised synchronisation is concretising – even though it is not the only reason.

To understand this phenomenon, I need to go back to what we were discussing earlier: mnemotechnics and mnemotechnologies. Previously, I described alphabetical writing as an orthothetic system that allows not only the literal recording of a discourse but also *a return* to the letter (and this is the theme of repetition that we have already introduced), and, by this possibility of return, to find from the same identified statement in the form of a text possible interpretations that are always more varied and diverse. This occurs according to the reading *context*: this one *de facto* overdetermines the interpretation since secondary retentions overdetermine the selection of primary retentions of a given temporal object. The reading context can vary according to two conditions: space and time. The reading of the same text at the same time in two different places gives two different interpretations. The reading of the same text in the same place but in two different epochs also varies. Again we find the production of differences in the repetition of the same.

Such is the literal orthotheticity. In *Symbols and Diabols*, I will show that the first goal of Plato's metaphysics is to eliminate this variability that he considers – wrongly, in my opinion – to be a threat to the city's unity. Plato denounces at a stroke poetry, arts and *hypomnesis* (that is, technics) in his fight against the plural interpretability of texts, the diversity of readings and the singularity that each citizen brings. I argue on the contrary that *anamnesis* is *essentially* interpretation, a text is by essence indefinitely interpretable: there can be no ultimate interpretation of a text. Nietzsche affirms, against Plato's horror for interpretation: the *endless* dimension of interpretation, and the irreducibility of multiple interpretations. This horror is also present amongst some contemporary Platonists.

The variability of interpretations is the manifestation of a great diachronicity in the reception of a text, since this reception is itself a process of interpretation. This diachronicity is itself the singularisation of the reader in the reading community that opens the text. This singularisation translates the realisation [*accomplissement*] of a process of individuation of this reader (a process in which the reader becomes who he is). At the same time, the unicity of the text, the identical establishing of its letter, is what supports a synchrony of singularities.

More specifically, the reader is first composed by the text of law: the citizen as a figure in ancient Greek is profoundly linked to the process of individuation that alphabetical writing made possible as an apparatus of '*différant* identity'. I therefore tried to produce concepts to formally account for the historical reality that was described at length by Jean-Pierre Vernant, Pierre Vidal-Naquet and Marcel Detienne.

We have seen that in the nineteenth century the arrival of analogic orthothetic technologies like the phonograph, and in the twentieth century the tape recorder [*magnétophone*], allows the recording of voices – like my own voice right now. These technics created the possibility of a real industry of temporal objects, since they consist, at first, in producing recording *machines*. With the literal synthesis, the scribe and the reader encoded and decoded the orthothetic recording, and any reader was potentially a scribe, while with the photographic apparatus, the phonograph, the cinematograph, the tape recorder and so on, it is the machines that are encoding and decoding. This made possible an industrialisation, since an industry is established from the separation of producers and consumers; this condition is fulfilled by the advent of analogic machines. While for the literal synthesis it is impossible to be a reader without knowing how to write (though not necessarily being a writer), it is possible for someone to receive an audiovisual image without having the skills to produce one.

The reversibility of the reader-scribe positions is the pledge [*gage*] of 'communitisation' that, for Husserl, opens the possibility of the transcendental *We* as a support, but it also opens the possibility of science as a dialogue between consciousnesses by means of 'reactivation' (as he calls it), or even the question of return, *Rückfrage*, which is a form of *anamnesis*. The sudden dissymmetry that arrives with the analogic mnemotechnologies breaks away from this horizon of literal tertiary retentions that support the promise of a communitisation, by substituting the 'isonomy' of citizens (their equality before the law, which is the juridical and political word for the so-called communitisation) with the *inequality* of producers and consumers created from a *new division of labour and social roles* by the deployment of machinism. This *symbolic inequality* is as serious as economic inequality, and both forms of inequality often come together. The former *relinquishes* individuals from their time, and thus from themselves.

Simondon has shown that the arrival of the tool-machine produced a *loss of individuation* of the worker, as he called it – the worker is deprived of his knowledge and reduced to the condition of being a servant to the machine that externalised his knowledge. The tool-machine becomes the 'technical individual', taking the worker's place; Simondon *de facto* reinterpreted analyses from Marx's manuscripts. With analogic technologies of temporal objects, a new loss of individuation is produced: it deprives the consciousnesses of their diachronicity, which is also their singularity.

I have demonstrated elsewhere that, to understand the necessity of this synchronisation of the industrial temporal objects, we need to understand the Industrial Revolution that happened in the nineteenth century and that led to a sudden proliferation of new objects connected in series, with the development of machinism. This industrial machinism presupposes huge investments from companies that therefore need to get a return on this ever greater immobilisation of capital. This necessity to invest is to increase surplus value and to guarantee amortisation of those investments made by companies that enter into increasingly fierce competition between themselves: to have access to innovation, to attract more capital, but also, and above all, to gain access to other markets to make the company profitable.

At the end of the twentieth century, and at the beginning of this twenty-first century, this competition has become a true global economic war that could – and we fear it with good reason – become a fully fledged war. From the nineteenth century, in order to amortise great machines of production, constituting the development of machinism, industries had to make mass products and produce ever newer products, bringing about slowly what became known as the consumer society. But they faced a problem: society does not spontaneously want to adopt these new industrial productions. The velocipedes, made by the Paris-based Compagnie parisienne des vélocipèdes, established in 1867, could only be socially adopted when several newspapers were launched (five specialised publications were created between 1880 and 1900, while *Le Petit Journal*, a high-circulation newspaper, had its own policy to promote bicycles), but were also advertised with competitions, and finally with the Tour de France, which continues to be highly mediatised. Even before showing achievements, the goal of these events was to convince future cyclists that it was possible to travel on two wheels without falling.

This imperative organised towards public opinion works at converting that opinion into a market of consumers by using all possible means to make it fantasise about the fetish-form of commodities. This is what the historian of technics Bertrand Gille calls the *permeabilisation* of social resistance to technological change. Almost all new industrial products are promoted by advertisement industries, and those industries are also engaged by cultural industries. Their role is to ease the adoption of innovative products by society – not only by socialising new behaviours, by inculcating new usages with these new products, but also by socialising the collective and social organisational models, which are also adapted to results from the industrial innovation (this is what Gille calls the problem of adjustment).[14] The modification of the behaviour of individuals who compose society is the first problem of industrial society, that they should no longer be called citizens but consumers: the *object* of consumption – the commodity – has become the main operator of the socialisation of individuals. In this way the media is essential to industrial democracies: as promoting innovation and vectors of the process of generalised adoption, central to capitalist modernity.

There have always been retentional apparatuses: we can call those who attempt to be in charge of the production of referential criteria for the selection of retention – for instance, by defining the educational models, the religious dogmas, the rules of law, and so on – 'the powers' [*les pouvoirs*].[15] But as long as the retentional authority is in the control of the cultural industries (amongst which I include information and telecommunication technologies), the process of selection is submitted to a *supreme criterion* that cannot be calculable; it is properly *incommensurable*. It is particularly true for the divine criterion but also for scientific truth, or the value of justice. While we know that justice on earth is a promise that will never be kept, and that *in practice* injustice rules, *by right* justice remains the *criterion* of all social behaviour, and we need to admit that justice is an *incommensurable* criterion. It cannot be the object of an evaluation according to a measurable and calculable reality, since reality is always *de facto* unjust. Yet it needs to be the *absolute* criterion. Similarly, in science, we cannot evaluate or calculate the truth value of a scientific statement by evaluating – I mean, by measuring – its value against other exchange values. We cannot claim that Thales' theorem is worth more than Pythagoras', and we cannot imagine a theorem gaining or losing value with time: we cannot speculate on (and calculate) such values, since they are absolute. And this is the case since the constitutive elements of the theorematic are idealities, as we discussed regarding lines and surfaces: these entities do not exist in the time and space of experience, but they constitute the very possibilities of experience. Equally for justice, realised justice does not exist and will *never* exist in experience: attempts to absolutely realise justice lead to hell, simply because justice is not a calculable object. However, it constitutes, as an ideality, the very possibility of a liveable experience. For this reason, justice is incommensurable: it is not measured in light of experience, and this is why 'market democracy' is an illusion. Justice cannot simply be the equilibrium of calculable behaviours of economic actors, and we cannot build a politics on the market. A politics, or, more generally, a psychic and collective individuation, can only entail a becoming-singular. And the market only produces the becoming-particular.

Incommensurability conditions all singularity, whether it is religious, political or other, whether it presents itself as the absolute authority of the 'father of all fathers' or as the ideality of a concept, and it is also the sign of artworks, but also of philosophy and eventually of all works of the 'spirit', as we call them. Yet this incommensurable difference between norms and facts, which needs *to be made*, is not given spontaneously and is strictly im-probable. It is in itself the responsibility of all consciousness, which is both in principle irreducible and *de facto* always threatened. By submitting retentional dispositifs to the market criteria, which always need to be subject to complex amortisement calculations, the very spirit is being purely and simply *liquidated*.

You understand now why I argued that, while I do not agree with Plato regarding his opposition between *anamnesis* and *hypomnesis* – since I believe that a certain practice of *hypomnesis* can make *anamnesis* possible (that is, the production of differences in repetitions) – I do however subscribe to this argument about the danger of *hypomnesis*, and that a hegemonic appropriation of *hypomnesis* (the retentional dispositifs) by economic forces governed by a purely financial logic is catastrophic, and it is this catastrophe that we are currently living.

Today, consciousnesses tend to synchronise, to adopt the same temporalities, and therefore lose their singularity. Yet consciousness is essentially a singularity in the sense that freedom is the act of consciousness par excellence. Consciousness par excellence – that is, *the acting out* of consciousness – is the freedom to think. To put it differently, what is threatened and systematically fought by this process of synchronisation is the philosophical potentiality of all consciousness. Philosophy is essentially the affirmation of the freedom of thinking that belongs to any consciousness, since it is intrinsically diachronic and therefore singular: it is thus potentially philosophising [*philosophante en puissance*]. What synchronisation tends to muffle is the potential to philosophise that belongs to all of us, and above all the possibility *to act out* this common potential that we all share, in particular as *a collective thought and political action*. This is possible since there is a profound stupidity in all consciousness that demands this synchronisation. Thinking is a struggle against stupidity, since when it prevails, laziness triumphs. Thinking is to fight one's own laziness. And this fight becomes harder and harder since the media is systematically exploiting and encouraging this laziness.

I am one of those who believe that it is possible to carry out a political action to increase the acuity of individual and collective consciousness, and to never renounce this vision and goal. I belong to those philosophers who proclaim this kind of acting out. This does not mean that I want to restore consciousness as the ground of thought and action. From the end of the nineteenth century, we have learned with Nietzsche, with Freud, with all Enlightenment's critiques of metaphysics, with the discovery of the role of systems and structures as well as the question of *praxis*, that consciousness is not its own master, that it hosts in itself forces that escape it. It is, as the host of spirit, inhabited by spirits that haunt it and ventriloquise it. It is precisely what I demonstrate with the concept of tertiary retention. But to take into account these points of view acquired in the twentieth century – and I believe them to be irreversible – cannot constitute an alibi to renounce a politics of consciousness as well as a political action – and, in particular, a politics that is conscious of the weakness of consciousness,[16] and what I have called elsewhere *the constitutive default of consciousness*. This default is a default of qualities, which is also a default of community constituting a community of default, as Bataille writes it. This is also what the myth of Prometheus and Epimetheus gives us to think.

Notes

1. [Trans.] Ludwig Wittgenstein, *Philosophical Investigations* (London: Blackwell, 2001).

2. [Trans.] On the historical role of orthothetics and orthographics, see Bernard Stiegler, *Technics and Time, Vol. 2: Disorientation*, trans. Stephen Barker (Stanford: Stanford University Press, 2008), pp. 57–64.

3. [Trans.] Sigmund Freud, *Civilization and its Discontents*, trans. James Strachey (New York: W. W. Norton and Company, 1989), p. 35.

4. [Trans.] G. W. F. Hegel, *Phenomenology of Mind*, trans. A. V. Miller (Oxford: Oxford University Press, 1977), p. 3, emphasis in the original.

5. [Trans.] Martin Heidegger, *Being and Time*, trans. John Macquarie and Edward Robinson (Oxford: Blackwell, 1978), H. 329, p. 378.

6. [Trans.] On melody and the temporal object in Husserl, see Stiegler, *Technics and Time, Vol. 2*, chapter 3 (pp. 188–243).

7. [Trans.] Henri Bergson, *Time and Free Will: An Essay on the Immediate Data of Consciousness*, trans. F. L. Pogson (New York: Dover, 2001).

8. [Trans.] See Xavier Lemarchand, 'Différance et audiovisuel numérique', PhD dissertation, Université de technologie de Compiègne, 1998; Bernard Stiegler, *Technics and Time, Vol. 3: Cinematic Time and the Question of Malaise* (Stanford: Stanford University Press, 2011), p. 15.

9. I use the conditional tense here since this story was later contested by François Albera.

10. I demonstrated in *Symbolic Misery, Vol. 1: The Hyperindustrial Epoch*, trans. Daniel Ross (Cambridge: Polity Press, 2014), that expectations are in general the expectation of the unexpected, and that the art of cinema consists in this reversal. This also applies to music.

11. Lucius Annaeus Seneca, *Letters from a Stoic*, trans. Robin Campbell (London: Penguin, 1969); Michel Foucault, 'Self Writing', in *Essential Works, Vol. 1: Ethics, Subjectivity and Truth*, ed. Paul Rabinow, trans. Robert Hurley and others (New York: The New Press, 2002), pp. 207–22.

12. [Trans.] See *Technics and Time, Vol. 2*, chapter 1, especially pp. 57–63.

13. [Trans.] Stephen Barker, the translator of *Disorientation*, translates *littérale* as 'literal' and 'literate' given the various meanings of 'literal' in English. Barker wants to note the opposition between the oral and the written, which is there in the French language but not in Stiegler since his work comes after Derrida's deconstruction of this opposition. However, 'literal' here should be understood in English in the material sense rather than in the metaphorical sense. See *Technics and Time, Vol. 2*, p. 248 n. 15.

14. On all these points, see Bernard Stiegler, *Technics and Time, Vol. 1: The Fault of Epimetheus*, trans. Richard Beardsworth and George Collins

(Stanford: Stanford University Press, 1998), especially pp. 34–7. Bertrand Gille, *The History of Techniques, Vol. 1: Techniques and Civilization*, trans. P. Southgate and T. Williamson (Montreux: Gordon and Breach Science Publishers, 1986), and *The History of Techniques, Vol. 2: Techniques and Sciences*, trans. J. Brainch and others (Montreux: Gordon and Breach Science Publishers, 1986).

15. I analysed this most in *Technics and Time, Vol. 3*.
16. This has nothing to do with what Gianni Vattimo called 'weak thought'. See Gianni Vattimo, *Weak Thought*, ed. Pier Aldo Rovatti, trans. Peter Carravetta (Albany, NY: State University of New York Press, 2013).

4. Consciousness, the Unconscious and the Unscience

ÉD: In referring to a political ecology of consciousness or spirit, amongst others, you distinguish the fundamental concepts of the synchronic/diachronic, or, to be more precise, synchronisation/diachronisation, as an opposed couple. It seems that the synchronisation of consciousnesses is closely tied to another general process that we can observe in all societies at the global scale: a process of uniformisation of behaviours and, more precisely, behaviours of consumption. But we are immediately tempted to object to the following: if we presuppose that indeed consciousnesses are synchronised by the hyperindustrial dispositif of production and broadcasting of temporal objects – which lead to a denial of agency to these consciousnesses [marge de manœuvre], or any possibility of diachronic subjectivation in the use of these objects (distracted listening, zapping and so on) – is it therefore legitimate to posit an a priori relation between synchronisation of consciousnesses and uniformisation of behaviours, without taking the time to question beforehand the sociological reality of this synchronisation? Do we really witness, especially in the case of temporal objects, a uniformisation of the modes of consumption? On the contrary, others would argue that markets are more and more segmented, and that consumption is increasingly moving towards an à la carte functioning, individualised, custom-made for ever more profiled users, according to criteria that allow combinations and diversified uses. We can take the examples made available by the internet, MP3 downloading, mobile phones with their own individualised ringtones, and so on. Earlier you noted that we do not listen in the same way, with the same attention and the same expectations, to a TV or radio show.

BS: We need to distinguish between two examples. If we listen to a quartet by Beethoven, each of us, in principle, not only listens singularly, but each of us, each time we listen to it, will listen to it again in a singular way. This diversity is not at all the same thing as the diversity of mobile phone ringtones that we are offered as an 'option', or all these options offered to us by the market segmentalisation: options for cars, options proposed by the travel industry to the tourist masses who believe to be going all over what they believe or no longer believe to be the world, or by the user profiling that also selects information that supposedly corresponds to your 'own personality'. The organisation of the market aims precisely at a systematic investment in all domains of life, absolutely all domains: leisure, education, old age and so on, far beyond the so-called 'material' consumer goods, and what we designate traditionally as services. The new form of capitalism takes into account all moments of individual existence – and consequently it defines all modes of social organisation, hence the imperative to liquidate states – to calculate and produce the *life-time value** as described by Jeremy Rifkin. This is done to standardise all behaviours, precisely by optimising them, and leading to the notorious industrial economies of scale. These options allow an artificial diversification since the programmes on generalist television all converge to the same model when they are subjected to the same market of audience figures.

The internet is perceived by large industry as an ideal system to read the hypersegmentation of markets. This means that there is an ever finer efficiency of marketing, with ever better defined and reached targets. The question is also that of speed and 'reactivity'. From the point of view of marketing, all these behaviours, even the most singular, need to be *anticipatable*, and therefore they are no longer *singular* behaviours, but *particular* behaviours.

Libido, which is absolutely indissociable from singularity,[1] can nonetheless be temporally diverted towards particularity, and advertising campaigns can favour those phantasmatic investments, but I think that libido *wears out* very quickly. Particularity refers here to the part of the partial object; this object is only the representative of the singular foundation needed for a particularity to exist. Hypersegmentation consists in substituting the singularity of my unique lifestyle [*mode de vie*], which resembles no other, with a particular behaviour belonging to a profilable list, a *check-list** corresponding to an industrial supply, and that is inscribed in what we call a profile, a *user profiling**.

Generally, consumption, in using and wearing out the libido, functions on the basis of an essential *frustration* – and produces a society of frustrated beings. The object consumed, precisely since it does not support singularity but folds it into particularity, is a deceptive object, and its consumption does not bring any satisfaction, does not support any pleasure; on the contrary, it intensifies the feeling of emptiness, vanity, that the consuming reaction strings together almost automatically ~~to attempt, in vain,~~ like Sisyphus, to fill in. In reality, he only intensifies this emptiness dully. He accumulates the conditions of generalised *disgust*.

One could believe that the internet network allows other modes of broadcasting, that it constitutes a new retentional dispositif, more open and alternative, as it were, to programming industries. In reality, this could be true if we managed to impose an entirely new organisational model to access information that this network of digital networks makes imaginable and realisable. As for me, I worked at the National Audiovisual Institute (INA), but also at the University of Compiègne, to define these alternative models. Unfortunately the models of access to information that dominate and structure the internet today are perfectly homogeneous with those of segmentation – in other words, responding to the logic of markets. If one wants to exist on the internet, if one wants to make a website, the important thing is obviously for this website to be visited. Yet it needs to be referenced and to adopt indexes and systems of content description that meet industrial standards: once again the imperative is to process huge masses and realise economies of scale. To be correctly referenced, the conditions of selection need to be anticipated in the individual production by the industrial retentional system.

There are, however, alternative solutions, and in this respect I developed two concepts: first, that of *authors' societies*, supported by what I called *situated semantics*, where communities of readers conceive, with electronic annotation systems, *thesaurii*, that is, *lists of authorities* that allow a very fine indexing by preserving the singular localities of indexing.[2] Second is the notion of the *discretisable audiovisual temporal object*,[3] which allowed the implementation of new audiovisual broadcasting dispositifs.[4]

Besides, one should not confuse the contemporary question of synchronisation with that of uniformisation, even though they have an immediate and evident relationship. Uniformisation is a fact, but it is far from being new. The uniform is a classical means to signal a belonging. It is also an incontestable fact that modernity is a new uniformisation. And it is also a fact that, for instance, Mao Zedong has made the Chinese people adopt a kind of uniform, and that this uniform denotes a kind of social alienation by a more or less coercive imposition of a behaviour, leading to stupidity and suffering – including the military uniform. Uniformisation is not only this. What I called earlier the *différant* identity presupposes a uniformisation: it is from this moment that the alphabet makes it possible to describe in a uniform manner a very large variety of idioms; these idioms were in turn made possible by the alphabet. Between these idioms, exchanges intensify their idiomatic content and their repetition leads to a difference through different interpretative experience, as I have previously described. But it should also be emphasised that alphabetic uniformisation – that Sylvain Auroux called 'grammatisation' – also produces true linguicides, liquidations of idioms. There is an entire political economy of uniformisation, as both entropic and negentropic. In *Symbols and Diabols*, I will try to show that these questions made up the history of an endless war of spirits, where grammatisation and more generally mnemotechnics constitute, with the retentional dispositifs, the very weapons of this war.

While the development of the alphabet has led to a perceptible liquidation of idiomatic diversities – for instance, Greek dialects – this uniformisation at the linguistic level by the alphabetisation has allowed a very strong diversification of individuals, an intensification of the singularity of individuating processes. Even though tribal idioms have without doubt disappeared with the development of the great lingua francas [*langues véhiculaires*], such as the Attic language of the Athenians that was strengthened by the adoption of a unique alphabet in 403 BC, speaking individuals could also assert in new ways their singularity when practising this novel way of speaking, constituted by the literate relation to language.

The uniformisation is therefore not in itself a bad thing. In other words, my answer is a way to show that I am not opposed to industry, on the contrary, nor am I an adversary of technology or modernity. I believe in the possibility of an industry that would not be fatally entropic. However, with today's mode of industrial development, with industrial policies [*politique industrielle*], or rather industrial non-policies, that devastate the contemporary world, we have come to the very limits of a process of lethal homogenisation.

Moreover, the synchronisation is of course not in itself a bad thing. Not only is it not a bad thing, but it is absolutely indispensable. For a society to be a society, dispositifs, structures and moments of synchrony need to exist. We need a synchronic horizon of the language if we want to speak to one another, as Ferdinand de Saussure explained. A language is a process of collective individuation that is carried on by all its speakers [*locuteurs*] at the same time, that is, it is carried to the limit of its equilibrium, or synchrony. Diachrony is a disequilibrium and synchrony is an equilibrium. Yet the fact of language – interlocution – is situated *in between* equilibrium and disequilibrium: it *tends* towards equilibrium *as much as* towards disequilibrium. *Provided that they do not simply engage in chattering*, any two persons will speak differently, that is, diachronically – otherwise, they would have nothing to say to one another. Speech is here an exchange of singularities and desires, as diachronies carrying *significance*, in their meeting, which is also *non-insignificance*.[5] This exchange produces novelty and also the crossing of a stage in psychic and collective individuation – the individuation of each speaker as well as the individuation of language itself. Language structures itself and *synchronises itself in new ways*.

In fact, for two speakers to converse, and exchange diachronies, as it were, a synchronic terrain of exchange needs to exist. But this terrain is always provisional and is never given as such. These two speakers begin in a given and already-there terrain, but when there is significance, a new terrain of synchrony is conquered. This new terrain can possibly only exist between these two speakers, in what forms a small idiolect, but it can also become an idiom, a way of speaking a language, shared by a group of speakers.

The problem is not synchrony in itself but the tendency to synchrony that governs all human exchange and, in particular, all interlocution. The problem raised by the current tendency to synchronisation is that it consists in a decomposition of the synchronic and the diachronic. A language is what articulates two tendencies, diachronic and synchronic, so they create a strong sense of belonging through strong synchronic links, but these would not find their power if it were not for the diachronic intensity that they make possible, that is, for the potential singularities and playing field these links open.

There is an 'ecological crisis of spirit' when the industrial control of synchrony leads to an opposition between the diachronic and the synchronic; when they de-compose, it is the process of psychic and collective individuation itself that decomposes. The *I* and the *We* get affixed into a *They* of idle talk, where there is nothing else to say, in the insignificance of the world: either you are synchronisable, but in renouncing your diachrony – that is, your singularity – you belong to the sphere of consumption and so-called 'modernity', or you are not synchronisable and you are marginal, deviant or even a terrorist; you are accused of asociality, even when this exclusive act *is* precisely the destruction of the social and relational.

We can object that in reality it does not happen this way. Indeed, we see behaviours that appropriate new technological processes and that, at the same time, develop a huge amount of singularity. I would be tempted to think of myself in this way. I would however invite sociologists who draw these kinds of conclusions to verify the magnitude of this observation: what sort of people are concerned, in what category of the population can these facts be proved, and to what extent do they not develop in the same way as the marginality that society lives and represses as asociability? As for me, I believe that we are in a deeply rifted society, to use a term that continues to be fashionable these days – for good reasons, unfortunately.[6] We live in a society in which, more and more, two worlds cohabit with more and more difficulty and improbability; they ignore one another in increasingly polarising and threatening ways. There is the world to which, *by chance* or *by accident*, I belong, along with many of those who listen to France Culture, many of them by chance as well. If they listen to France Culture, which has not yet become an organ of definite cretinisation, it is because they resist this tendency, at least partly. But let's not delude ourselves: *no one* can escape this tendency. Directly or indirectly, we are subjected to it, if only the tendency to escape instinctually from the vile [*immonde*], and therefore the *ignorance* – or what I called earlier 'the unscience' – that we hold so dear in front of facts.

If, by chance, some people continue to be in a culture of singularities – and I hope I belong to this culture as well – there are still *countless* people who live in entirely different, and often extremely alienating, working conditions; when they have work, it is in entirely destructured urban environments, which are the result of a functional urbanism that separated residential from commercial neighbourhoods, shops from business centres, and so on, leading to literally *unliveable* zones. I know these zones very well: I spent my childhood in them, at Sarcelles, and already at that time we called it 'sarcellite' – inhabitants of the uninhabitable are the privileged targets of supermarkets, publicists, PR entities that sell commodities with 'options', banks that sell loans and interest rates, and so on.

These people live in another world, close to the vile [*immonde*], a kind of non-world, or somewhere that *tends* towards a non-world – something like hell. I am not saying that nothing can come out of it: I left a passage very close to the vile. I am trying to say that nothing good can come out of ignoring this fact, or minimising it, from the side of those who leave it or by those who think that their unscience allows them to leave this fact behind. I think that when we make sociological analyses, we need to take into account these two worlds. Let's not delude ourselves into making the hypothesis of a common world; this is an entirely abstract fiction of an academic or media-based discourse that only works to legitimise the established disorder.

Of course, there are – and fortunately so – some bridges between these two worlds, their opposition comes with different gradations, some of us belong to both worlds, depending on where we are, the activities that we have, the moments of the day we live. I try to cultivate in my own existence, whenever I can, some of these passages, and therefore I try to belong to both worlds. Our society is more and more split, and a part of it has sunk into hypersynchronisation, and it has lost a major part of its self-esteem and is close to eruption since the situation is in all respects unbearable, but more importantly – and this is far worse – it is symbolically unbearable. It leads to the danger of reversing symbols into what I call *diabols*, and a risk taken by an era obsessed with the diabolical.

It is this symbolic dispositif that has made the unity of a society. Until the nineteenth century, the symbolic dispositif was the fruit of clerics. Clerics make up a category, whether they are religious, secular or simply 'intellectuals', which is not involved in economic activity and production. They are in charge of producing symbols of collective belonging, constitutive of the *We*. They produce the synchronic horizons, that is, the common spaces of experimentation of individual singularities, as artists, as intellectuals, as religious persons, as jurists and so on. These common spaces of experimentation that I am referring to are the dispositifs of repetition that give difference.

While until the end of the nineteenth century the world of clerics had continued to be distinct from the world of production, by the early twentieth century these two worlds began to merge. The clerics are absorbed by the world of production: they disappear. This is what leads to the systematic exploitation of symbolic production, entirely subjected to the market criteria. These are purely immanent, utilitarian and calculable criteria – but at the same time they are deprived of the strength and symbolic efficiency that inhabit the works of spirit. This is what Hannah Arendt discusses when she raises the question of 'durability'.[7]

When the production of symbols becomes reduced to an effect from calculation, and consequently the symbol is amortisable in the short term, the production of symbols should now be understood *as selection criteria* subjected to the archi-criterion of profitability in the short term: then symbols are reversed into *diabols*. I define symbols as secondary and

tertiary retentions of the *We* that make the selection of primary retentions possible in the everyday flow.

The difficulty is *to avoid diabolising the diabol*. The diabol is also what
produces individual singularity. The diabol sides with the diachronic. In
a way, it is Plato who diabolises the diabol. The diabol is the dynamic
and paradoxical principle of a healthy synchronic: this is what Simondon
calls the dephasing of the individuating process that *ensures the movement*
of this individuation, as the tendency to disequilibrium present in metastability. It comes at a moment when the criteria become immanent and
are hegemonically subjected to calculations, where diabols and symbols
are entirely separated. We enter this vileness and, in this sense, into the
possibility of the diabolical. When the decomposition of the symbolic
leads to a de-composition of the synchronic and the diachronic, a reversal of the symbols and diabols takes place, bringing about a strictly diabolical situation: far from constituting the process of projecting the unity
of a *We*, in a welcoming and desired synchrony, the symbol produces a
loss of self-esteem and social atomisation that can lead to war – either
civil or military war.

*ÉD: Do you think that a politics of culture can play a role in this 'diabolic' landscape?
Since what is at stake is symbolic, is it not a politics of symbols that we would need?
Perhaps we do not need a politics that only plays out in the symbolic domain – which
unfortunately makes our everyday – but a form of symbolic ecology that would redefine
the domain of the political?*

BS: All politics is also a politics of symbols, sometimes the worst and
sometimes the best symbols. Regarding the fleshing out of a politics
worthy of the situation, I believe that a new critique of consciousness is
necessary. As I have already explained, at the beginning of the twentieth
century, we denounced with reason the illusions of 'awareness' [*prise de
conscience*] and mastery as conceived by the philosophies of consciousness. My work on technics, and the relation between *anamnesis* and
hypomnesis, raises the irreducible character of what we call the passive
synthesis – a synthesis that is made outside the subject, in contrast with
his or her judgement and decision that are called 'active synthesis'. But
it does not mean that this approach renounces consciousness, since this
would simply be renouncing philosophy and thought as such, and, with
that, renouncing freedom and the very possibility of decision. We cannot
deny that contemporary melancholia can help us perceive the contem-

porary situation, even though we can be tempted to take pleasure in this very melancholia; we cannot escape it. But we should not concede to this. The right to thinking should be affirmed, the duty of acting out.

At this stage, I find it necessary to rethink in depth what consciousness is. Until the end of the nineteenth century, up until Nietzsche, consciousness is thought of as the spiritual sphere, as the non-material, as the immaterial. (Marx is a special case: when he refers to 'class consciousness', he does not argue very much about consciousness even while denouncing its metaphysical conception; in Engels, consciousness is reduced to the question of dialectics.) Consciousness, from the fundamental opposition introduced by Plato between material-mortal body and immaterial-immortal soul, is always conceived as philosophy in its opposition between matter and form, what Simondon has definitively critiqued by thinking technics.

I try to think with concepts such as epiphylogenesis, where consciousness is a form of life and a series of decisions, or tertiary retention, where memory is always already hypomnesically constituted and with it records not only consciousness but also the *unconscious*. Therefore I try to think consciousness as being essentially constituted by the time of consciousness itself, constituted by tertiary retentions, forming each time a world that is also a *historical-technical milieu of spirit*.

To come back to the beginning of our interview, what makes who I am is the manner in which I have inherited a past that I have not lived. I have inherited a spirit that haunts me, which was received from the experience of my ancestors, which we call culture, and that led to ways of living that constitute my own past, my lived past. This legacy and my lived past are made accessible *via* tertiary retentions, and this takes place ever since the Australopithecus, although in different ways: tertiary retentions transform themselves and transform humans' relations to time, and they transform the human itself, which is only a relation to time. The first condition is narcissism and the 'mirror stage' that Lacan refers to, and I argue that this first condition is understood precisely in tertiary relations.

The layer of tertiary retentions is constitutive of the human and it has become the field of systematic industrial exploitation, ruining the processes of consciousness (as nodes of singularities capable of taking decisions), but also ruining desire, as processes of unconsciousness – if I can put it this way. To fight this state of affairs, one needs to rethink in depth the material condition of consciousness as well as the unconscious. I am a materialist since I posit that consciousness is constituted by matter; but I am also a spiritualist, since I posit that matter supports spirits that are not reducible to matter, and that haunt consciousness from the unconscious. Consequently, I practise a spiritual materialism or a materialist spiritualism. From this position, I call for a new critique of consciousness as well as the unconscious that would ground once again a political project, or that would allow us to face a passage beyond politics, beyond Western individuation. One needs to ask whether the very word 'politics' is adequate: *polis* is indeed very far from us. This is why when we argue for the necessity to think action, in order to maintain the possibility of a *We*, including in its articulation with an *It* (in other words, the *It* denotes what makes the *criterion improbable* in its symbolic power and irreducible to calculation), the word 'politics' would only be appropriate at the cost of a critique, and especially a critique of law, which remains to be done.

After all, Kant or Condorcet, but before them Rousseau and Diderot, opened 'Enlightenment', that is, the discourse on consciousness as the condition of a political revolution. 'Political revolution' does not necessarily mean terror and beheading, and it does not simply mean awareness [*prise de conscience*] either: it should also be an unawareness [*prise d'inconscient*]. To start a revolution does not necessarily mean fire and blood: to start a revolution essentially consists in positing that *an era is over* [*révolue*] and that something else should come instead. The words 'era', 'positing' and how 'something else should come' need to be questioned. I can 'posit' that this revolution lies in the uttering of this sentence; in this case it does not translate into anything in reality, except in a new tertiary retention! But if this is the case, I produce a revolutionary writing, which will perhaps one day be translated into revolutionary *acts* and decisions.

Something else should come, that is, new modes of thinking that no longer oppose, for instance, the material and the spiritual, and to me this is a revolutionary position. This means that we need to think the symbolic (and the *I*, and the *We*, and the narcissisms that support them) without opposing the diachronic and the synchronic, while continuing to re-evaluate in depth the great concepts inherited from philosophy, and not abandoning them, but *critiquing them, especially in light of all the questions linked to the development of technoscience in the twentieth century and the new problems associated with this development, as a working hypothesis.*

The Industrial Revolution established a new relation between science and technics that is relatively poorly analysed by the great thinker of technical revolution, Marx. At the very beginning of our interview, I argued that philosophy, as an *epistēmē* that could be clearly distinguished from science, was opposed to technics. It is a general truth that ever since Plato until around the eighteenth century, science and technics were not only separated but strictly opposed. Yet this situation started to change with the Industrial Revolution that began in England. All of a sudden, science was associated with technics for the needs of industry and it changed meaning entirely. From a science which had the ambition to tell the state of things – that is, identity, essence and stability – we move towards a science that seeks to explore the possible becomings of things. It is much less interested in the real than in the possible, much less in being than in becoming.

Today, instead of being opposed, by associating itself with technics, science becomes a kind of science fiction: a science capable of producing chimeras. This situation is a total upheaval in the conceptual apparatus that philosophy used to think science, politics, aesthetics and religion, roughly between Plato and Kant. To this day we have not yet evaluated what this becoming-technoscience of science means. We have not yet measured the degree of engagement of science in the world, and it is far from being a simple neutral objectivation [*objectivation*] of processes, becoming an actor of these processes. Yet this position of actor is a central epistemic change.

In particular, we do not understand the debate around genetically modified organisms (GMOs) and the associated reactions; especially in France, when farmers are condemned for their actions, the gestures of the farmers' association (*Confédération paysanne*) are reminiscent of peasant revolts [*jacqueries*] and manifest a certain lucidity regarding the changing status of science. We bury our heads in the sand when we call these demonstrators vandals, as Dominique Lecourt declared.[8] These 'vandals' denounced the processes that resulted from the changes of direction of science but that have not been evaluated. These farmers demand with reason that we discuss the transformation of science and the exclusively industrial finalities that drive it. Here again, *it is a question of control of memory*, but this time *biological* memory is concerned, be it vegetal, animal or human, as the object of a tertiarisation and the industrial control of a new retentional dispositif that Foucault analysed as biopower.

What is happening to the production of transgenic plants like GMOs, for instance, or with human cloning? We cannot ignore the fact that the techno-industrial development constitutes a *unilateral decision of selection among all possibles* of the technicised living. Such a development is hegemonically subjected, once again, to the criterion of short-term profitability: nothing can be more entropic and hostile to life, which is by essence negentropic. We cannot ignore the fact that *the selection criteria of possibles have nothing scientific*: they are purely economic and capitalist.

It is deeply unjust to simply call José Bové a vandal, to get rid of the serious problem he presents us, and to give him a fourteen-month prison sentence. We cannot call him a vandal because he is opposed to the situation towards which we are blindly directing ourselves. He is right to denounce it. He is, however, wrong to do it by targeting laboratories. Like Dominique Lecourt, I condemn this by principle. Yet at the same time, I cannot ignore the fact that José Bové and the *Confédération paysanne* know that a media presence is necessary and, unfortunately, the very working of the media apparatus requires sensational behaviour and the creation of a commotion that will be heard.

Instead of denying all legitimacy to the discourse of José Bové and his friends, we need to critique it: their arguments are meagre, they denounce the 'technical system' with Jacques Ellul's concepts, which seem insufficient to me. But on the other hand, not to take into account what Ellul has pointed out, that technics is the 'challenge of the century', is as worrying as the crude denunciation that too often stands for critique, while in truth it really empties out any possibility of critique.

Concerning the question of GMOs, I do not really know what to think except that, first, it is the biopolitical dimension of the question of selection and the industrial retentional dispositifs. Second, I cannot imagine how earth will face the huge demographic problems to come without adopting new food production techniques. However, I do not trust the current state of the industry to hand over the future of retentions and their selection, and determine the living.

A profound epistemological, philosophical, scientific, aesthetic, economic and political revolution should take place in our minds as well as in our acts. In this respect, there is a kind of blindness among certain scientists, and in a way it is not only the unscientific state of science but, above all, the disavowal [*dénégation*] of this unscience and, with it, the denial of the unconsciousness that this worrying situation creates. This situation encourages rejections, reactivity and *ressentiment* that proliferate in different forms throughout the world. By becoming technoscience, science explores and realises possibles as fictions, *in the sense that all artefacts are partly linked to fiction*: it becomes science fiction, and is no longer guided by a truth criterion derived from the sky of ideas – the models that essences made in Platonism. This means that the depth of the question of fiction needs to be reconsidered, along with its relation to truth. I tried, in my own work, to draw out consequences from the passage of a science conceived as a description of being to a science conceived as the inscription of new possibles (and thus constituted as technoscience, strictly speaking). The question is not to refuse this becoming. Eventually, this becoming only deploys what is contained in the originary hypomnesic character of all knowledge. The question, however, is that of knowing how to distinguish between good and bad fictions, to learn *to think a truth that would not be opposed to fiction, but a truth composed with fictions.* This is perhaps related to the theological question, since it often designates God as a necessary fiction. I'm not calling for a return of the theological; I feel far away from this idea – even though I believe that we need to rethink entirely the religious question since we have not come to terms with it. I raise the question of God in terms of *diabelein.*

I ask the scientific community to take into account *as much as possible* the absolutely novel character of these questions, as well as the prudence that they call for. I understand this word ('prudence') as a translation of Aristotle's concept of *phronēsis.*[9] The Aristotelian prudence raises a problem, however, precisely due to his conception of *technē* that does not allow taking contemporary technology into consideration. This problem is even greater in Kant, for whom technics is simply applied science.[10] I therefore demonstrated that it is no longer possible to think technics in this perspective. Unfortunately, in spite of the questions opened by Bachelard concerning, for instance, the role of the technological in scientific experience, philosophers and many scientists often think or do not think technics with this archaic Kantian concept (and Alexis Philonenko understood this very well).

The disavowal of these problems by scientists is, in truth, for me a form of *ressentiment,* and the reactivity that grows in the world. An axiomatic revolution of our minds and acts is the first step towards the accomplishment of an 'ecology of spirit' that knows *as much as possible* the extent (and the excessiveness) of (1) the *constitutive* place of technics, that arrives in all domains – from the exploitation of the raw material of our conscious time [*temps de conscience*] by cultural industries or by exploitation of the biological molecules transformed into mnemotechnic materials; and (2) the way in which financial power seized technics hegemonically, by understanding it empirically *de facto* although missing out on its *de jure* direction [*sens*]; it has therefore ignored the limits of its actions that will be made self-evident at some point, but perhaps too late.

I understand the practice of *critiquing* after Kant as the task of *limiting* or *delimiting*. This critique, this political economy of symbols, spirits and living bodies that inhabit these spirits, needs to show the suiciding dimension, as it were, for capital, as well as the drive for an unlimited and uncritiqued exploitation of consciousnesses and bodies. All of this leads to disarray and to the liquidation of narcissism and desire, but more problematically it will end up annihilating the market itself.

Moderation [*mesure*] and immoderation [*démesure*] are indissociable. It therefore requires us to return to the tragic sense: something that Nietzsche had already invited us to do. It does not mean that we need to return to a pre-Platonic Greek thought, but that we should read the Greeks who came before Plato without interiorising everything that is Pauline in his way of thinking (it has been noted that Paul was the translation of Plato into Judaism and as such the invention of Christianity). The tragic philosophers thought without opposition, this is what Nietzsche taught us: they thought the tragic situation as composition, or, to put it differently, the irreducibility of fiction. We come after Christianity, we need to revisit the withering Christian history of the West [*Occident*] from the point of view of the tragic: this history began as a departure from the tragic and as the *forgetting* of its sense. We are in charge of this *reminiscence*. This is the immense strength of Bertrand Bonello's film *Tiresia* that brings a sensibility to these questions that appear at first abstract.[11]

To put it differently, in passing through the question of the tragic, the critique that I am referring to consists in *thinking the accident* first, and the accidental origin of human fate; thinking and *philosophising* the accident and *with* the accident, if I can put it this way, and therefore *by* accident, otherwise it would contribute to reactive discourses.

Notes

1. On this point, see Bernard Stiegler, 'To Love, To Love Me, To Love Us: From September 11 to April 21', in *Acting Out*, trans. David Barison, Daniel Ross and Patrick Crogan (Stanford: Stanford University Press, 2008), pp. 37–8, and *Symbolic Misery, Vol. 1: The Hyperindustrial Epoch*, trans. Daniel Ross (Cambridge: Polity Press, 2014).
2. These concepts are derived from the work I did for the National Library in France (BNF) in 1990.

3. I presented this concept on different occasions, particularly in the article 'La numérisation des objets temporels', in Franck Beau, Philippe Dubois and Gérard Leblanc (eds), *Cinéma et dernières technologies* (Paris: INA/De Boeck, 1998).

4. This is what the studio of hypermedia production that I created in 1997 at the INA continues to use today; it is directed by Jean-Pierre Mabille and his assistant Xavier Lemarchand.

5. [Trans.] Cornelius Castoriadis also wrote on insignificance in two books: the untranslated *The Rising Tide of Insignificance* in 1996 and *Postscript on Insignificance: Dialogues with Cornelius Castoriadis*, ed. Gabriel Rockhill, trans. Gabriel Rockhill and John V. Garner (London: Continuum, 2011).

6. [Trans.] The expression 'rifted society' echoes Jacques Chirac's famous slogan for the 1995 presidential elections, the 'social rift' (*la fracture sociale*). A recent controversial sociological study on the French working classes continued this argument; see Christophe Guilly, *Fractures françaises* (Paris: Flammarion, 2013).

7. [Trans.] Hannah Arendt, *The Human Condition* (Chicago: University of Chicago Press, 1998), pp. 136–7, 167–8.

8. [Trans.] Dominique Lecourt (1944–) is a French historian and philosopher of science at the University Paris 7 Saint-Denis, and the director of the Centre Georges Canguilhem. He first worked with Althusser and Canguilhem in the tradition of French historical epistemology, and later wrote on contemporary topics such as cloning, bioethics, posthumanism, mythology and the politics of fear. See François Ewald and Dominique Lecourt, 'Les OGM et les nouveaux vandales', *Le Monde*, 3 September 2001.

9. See Aristotle, *Nicomachean Ethics*, 2nd edn, trans. Terence Irwin (Indianapolis: Hackett Publishing, 1999), book 6, chapter 5, pp. 89–90, and Pierre Aubenque, *La Prudence chez Aristote* (Paris: Presses Universitaires de France, 1963).

10. All these questions are analysed in detail in 'The Malaise of Our Educational Institutions', in Bernard Stiegler, *Technics and Time, Vol. 3: Cinematic Time and the Question of Malaise*, trans. Stephen Barker (Stanford: Stanford University Press, 2011), pp. 131–56.

11. [Trans.] For a commentary of this film, see 'Tiresias and the War of Time: On a Film by Bertrand Bonello', in Stiegler, *Symbolic Misery, Vol. 1*, pp. 81–93.

Appendix 1. The Technologisation of Memory: Interview with Élie During

Élie During (ÉD): In your view, the culture industry's mass production of temporal objects is inseparable from a 'mass-produced temporalisation of consciousness'. How does this remark represent a new take on the question of mass Kulturindustrie *as formulated by the Frankfurt school? In other words, what is the difference between what you say about Hollywood as 'the world capital of schematism', and Adorno and Horkheimer's denunciation of an alienation mechanism in which 'cars, bombs and films ensure the system's cohesion'?*

Bernard Stiegler (BS): What limits Horkheimer and Adorno's analysis is that in denouncing the process of the technical exteriorisation of the imagination, they fail to explain why consciousness can be so highly penetrated and controlled by the unfolding of a movie or a temporal object in general. In order to grasp the problem, we have to start with an exact definition of the concept of temporal object. What I call a temporal object is one whose flow coincides with the flux of the consciousness of which it is the object, and which therefore is basically a flux itself, since it exists only with the passage of time, as a flow. The paradigm for such a thing is a melody, as Husserl demonstrated. A temporal object is woven of retentions and protentions. These protentional and retentional processes also weave the temporality of consciousness in general – and by the same token temporal objects make it possible to modify these processes of consciousness, and, to some extent, to influence or even control them. These processes are most highly formalised in music, which explains, for example, its military and religious functions.

ÉD: How exactly do you see the relationship between temporal objects and retentional processes? And how do you go from there to the question of the alienation of consciousness?

BS: In the 'now' of a melody, in the present moment of a musical object in its unfolding, the note played can only be a note (i.e. not just a sound) insofar as it retains within itself the preceding note, and the still-present preceding note retains the one before that, which in turn retains the previous note, etc. This primary retention, which pertains to the present of perception, shouldn't be confused with secondary retention, which is, for example, a melody I may have heard last night, which I can play back in my imagination through the workings of memory, and which constitutes the past of my consciousness. Husserl tells us that we shouldn't confuse perception (primary retention) with imagination (secondary retention). Before the invention of the phonograph it was absolutely impossible to hear exactly the same melody twice in a row. The advent of sound recording, which is itself what I have called a 'tertiary retention' (a prosthesis, exteriorised memory), made possible the identical repetition of the same temporal object, and that allows us to better understand the importance of retentional processes. On the one hand, when the same temporal object is repeated twice in a row, it gives rise to two different temporal phenomena, which means that the primary retentions are different in each of them: the retentions of the first hearing become secondary and play a selective role in the primary retentions during the second hearing. But on the other hand, tertiarised temporal objects, that is, recordings (phonograms, films, radio and television broadcasts), are materialised time overdetermining the relationship between primary and secondary retentions, and making it possible to control them in some respects. Today, the flux of consciousness of which we are constituted increasingly follows the rhythm and warp of precisely these kinds of mass-produced temporal objects. With the technological changes now under way, we are going from an industrial stage to what could be called a hyperindustrial stage, which integrates the world of culture and the mind in its entirety into an enormous technological-industrial system where the same machinery produces material goods and disseminates symbols and other forms of 'spiritual nourishment'. Moreover, TV receivers are now being transformed into remote control terminals, allowing us not only to watch programmes but to perform actions at a distance, such as purchases, now, and many other things in the future. This is leading to a general synchronisation of the temporal flow of consciousness, something which will develop more and more.

ÉD: The idea that we are experiencing a process of uniformisation linked to the globalisation of the systems of cultural production and dissemination (a process accelerated by the establishment of standards of interoperability between digital infrastructures) usually arouses either admiration or condemnation, moralisation or thrilled futurology. How does your thinking relate to the standard critical discourse on globalisation?

BS: To respond adequately to that question, we'd have to go back to the thinkers who have been considering it for the last two hundred years. An amazing amnesia surrounds it today, as if Braudel, for example, had never written on the subject, or as if the Marxian analysis of capital was not primarily concerned with globalisation. In my view, the question of globalisation is directly linked to the development of the technical system. Globalisation means, above all, that the technical system of production of symbols as well as material goods is now starting to operate on a world level. From the West to the Far East there's been an enormous shift – the power of symbolic production, formerly in religious, artistic, political and intellectual hands, is now subordinated to and integrated into the industrial and sales apparatus and its criteria; the technical system has entirely absorbed the mnemotechnical system. From the Neolithic period through to the nineteenth century, the rhythm and conditions of development of the latter were structurally distinct from the technological system for the production of material goods: the writing of the alphabet remained the same even though the technological systems of production changed constantly. For the last thirty years an integration of the two systems has been under way, and now, in 2001, it is complete.

ÉD: In your book, you warn of the danger of a 'loss of individuation', and the subtitle refers directly to the question of ill-being, an existential malaise. It's hard to take this as mere medical diagnosis and not see it as a moral evaluation . . .

BS: The point is not to condemn a process or construct an edifying philosophy, but to analyse the existing facts and from that consider the possibility of right (in the sense that Kant distinguishes the question of fact and the question of right, or *de facto* and *de jure*). The integration of the technical system and mnemotechnics is a fact, a very long-term process to which any 'resistance' would be an illusion. Leroi-Gourhan summarises this trend by a concept that I have adopted: exteriorisation. But this process opens up various alternative possibilities; it's not a matter of blind determinism. A number of questions of political economy arise within this framework, and they are still rather ill-defined because we don't distinguish between becoming, the process overall, and time, what we do with the process. This process actually requires us to make choices, to make a distinction, even though at first, taken simply as a becoming, it might seem to consist of a general elimination of difference, what I've called synchronisation. The production of difference can only arise from a critique of that which within the process goes against the process itself. The conclusion of this process (its end and liquidation) must be diverted in time, time which generates difference. That's what I call invention. I think any resistance to the future is irrelevant. The point is not so much to resist it as to invent it, or in other words to transform it into time: the invention of differences which bring out the new within a process that in and of itself tends, on the contrary, to eliminate them. In *Technics and Time, Vol. 2: Disorientation*, my general intention was to show how the process we are seeing has resulted in disorientation, in the sense that we have completely lost our sense of North, East and West and are experiencing a global confusion leading to suicidal and other extreme behaviours. What's needed in the face of the process of the integration of technics and mnemotechnics is a critical reformulation making it possible to make distinctions which aren't given in advance, so that we can get our bearings. That's why I wrote a commentary of Kant's 'What Does It Mean to Orient Oneself in Thinking?'.[1] Today we're in a situation where we have to decide between possibles which are all fictions, to differentiate between good and bad fictions. In the end, philosophy is always based on the idea that you have to differentiate. But until now, it considered fiction a bad difference, and tended to contrast it to the true, taken as the non-fictional. But if, as we see with tertiary phonographic retentions, secondary retention always plays a role in the selection of primary retentions, this means that perception always works with the imagination, that reality is therefore always projected by the imagination: fiction is a component of consciousness. So, the point is to be able to differentiate between good and bad fictions. Systematic industrial exploitation of our consciousness leads to a very bad fiction, one that kills our powers of imagination, desire and fictionalising.

ÉD: How does this disorientation pose a political question? I have the impression that the way you get to the root of the problem through a reconsideration of the question of retention inherently leads to politics. What you call 'the cinema of consciousness' (the

hypothesis that consciousness, in general, is cinematographic in and of itself) would
necessarily be a political cinema . . .

BS: Absolutely. Consciousness does work like a movie projector; not
only a projector but also a machine for capturing, recording, splic-
ing, editing, post-production, mixing and special effects. The movies
are an exteriorisation of the structure of consciousness. Consciousness
is a cutting room, a central control room, because it edits the flow of
primary, secondary and tertiary retentions. I say this on the basis of
Husserl and a close reading of the triple synthesis of the imagination
presented in the *Critique of Pure Reason*. The concept of retention is essential in order to understand the political problem posed by the process
of the integration of technics and mnemotechnics. Retention is what
allows us to retain the past in the present for the future. The memory
in the nerves of my cerebral cortex performs this retention. But there is
also the retention of the present within the present (Husserl's primary
retention) and the artificial, exteriorised memory held by a trace or an
object (tertiary retention). A carved flint is a form of recording, a manual
activity, as are writing, photography, phonographs, signs scribbled into
a diary, words spoken into a tape recorder, and a knot in my handker-
chief. In each of these examples, we put symbolic elements into material form so that they can be preserved through time. The process of
hominisation is essentially linked to this possibility of tertiary retention,
because these materialised symbolic memorisations are what makes it
possible to transmit an individual's memory to the collective. The future
of societies and the very possibility of the existence of a *We* are overde-
termined by these retentional mechanisms. But every retentional technology also applies criteria for retention or selection. Clearly everything
can't be retained; memory can only function if it is selective (the paradox
described by Borges in 'Funes, His Memory').[2] So the political question
is always this: what are society's criteria for retention? Totalitarianism is
characterised by hegemonic selection criteria. Law itself is the choice of
a form to make case-by-case decisions on the basis of variable elements.
That is what gives law its general applicability. The judgement of ideas,
what's called universality, rests on the possibility of an infinity of judge-
ments through time; there is a particular economy of selection where the
criterion is the possibility of universalisation and thus infinitisation. Until
the twentieth century, all this was produced, *de jure* and *de facto*, by the
circle of clerics, which was relatively independent of the constraints of

the sphere of material production and business. Today this is no longer the case, because the process of retention has itself become material. When the British Paramount archives, including their newsreels, are bought up by VisNews and most of them are destroyed because the film stock they are recorded on is highly inflammable, the imperative guiding the company, which comes from the stockholders, is to obtain the fastest possible return on their investment. The sphere of the marketplace applies a criterion that is no longer that of the universal infinitisation of a judgement but the most rapid amortisation possible. In contrast, the imperative of universalisation implies the slowest amortisation possible. There is a radical conflict between these criteria, because the mind is not amortisation. The mind does not pay off.

ÉD: What is the exact nature of the link you indicate between the mass production of programmes and the homogenisation of the criteria of retention? How is it that second-ary retentions, which are filters, tend to become homogenised (as do consciousnesses as well, by the same token)?

BS: When ten million people watch the same broadcast, the same audio-visual temporal object, they synchronise their fluxes. Of course, the criteria they apply for retention are different, and so they don't all per-ceive the same phenomenon or think the same thing about what they're seeing. When I listen to a melody for a second time, I don't hear exactly the same thing, in the sense that my listening is not the same – which shows, by the way, how technics makes possible differentiation and not just homogenisation. The original protentions are no longer present; I've already 'refilled' them and now I have a secondary retention (a memory) of the object which in fact serves to filter primary retentions. The secondary retention is what explains the difference between the two hearings. But while the secondary retentions shape the selection criteria at work in primary retentions, the fact that every day the same people watch the same shows necessarily leads them, in the end, to share the same secondary retentions, and thus to select the same primary retentions. They end up being so much in synch that they lose their diachrony, i.e. their singularity, and in the last analysis their freedom to think.

ÉD: But we are often told that the new digital technologies and the increasing segmen-tation of the markets of cultural goods will bring about more diversification, with à la carte programming making it possible for people to choose what they see, personalised viewing, artworks on command, etc.

BS: In 1987, at the Centre Georges Pompidou, I curated the exhibition *Memories of the Future*, which was an attempt to create a space to play out possible alternatives created by contemporary memorisation technologies. The ecology of networks and archives always occasions amazingly naive discourses. As Rifkin demonstrated in *The Age of Access*, the question with networks is access.[3] The filters are what counts. Today, search engines that make it possible to hierarchise information charge people for being referenced. It's always a question of selection. User profiling consists in identifying your search behaviours so that you can be offered things before it even occurs to you to ask for them. If this doesn't amount to consciousness programming, it's at least Pavlovian conditioning and reinforcement. You are locked into your synchronicity, prevented from changing, in an effort to achieve hypersegmentation, a marketing strategy that consists in identifying marketing micro-niches. Thus behaviours are standardised by reducing them to socio-professional categories or 'tribes' identified by 'markers' that are far more useful for marketing than political society. The media use mass-production consciousness-exploiting technologies by imposing their criteria for retention. The effect of this control of retentional mechanisms where consciousnesses represent a market (the value of an hour of consciousness is equal to the total cost of the ad time divided by the number of viewers, which comes to a few cents) is the homogenisation of secondary retentions. This is one essential cause (but not the only one) of our existential malaise. Control over our retentions implies a loss of identity, which means of difference. Nietzsche clearly saw this loss of the ability to produce difference and the tendency for societies to negate the exception. Our supposedly individualistic societies are in reality completely herd-like.

ÉD: Does this bring back the romantic figure of the individual genius who creates himself and new values?

BS: No, my discourse on singularity has nothing to do with autonomy. I posit technics, society and exteriority in general as among its constituent elements. My starting point is not consciousness but technics, which is not a ground but an initial 'groundlessness' [*effondement*] which I have also called the default of origin. I am not saying that what we have to get back to is the singularity of the romantic self – rather, it's the process of individuation, in Simondon's sense of the term. Individuation is always simultaneously psychic and collective. The *I* exists only insofar as it is part of the individuation of the *We* through that which links the former to the latter, namely mnemotechnologies, tertiary retentions. Today this *We* is in trouble; we don't know who's saying *We*. The *We* is fraying at the edges, becoming unbounded. The abrupt change in our retention technologies means that we have no understanding of our retention criteria.

ÉD: How do you see the role of art in this context?

BS: Art establishes a slice of time. It is an event, a suspension and an invention. It makes the synchronic diachronic. It is a reverse entropic factor, and its effect should be reconsidered in the framework of an overall energetic and symbolic evaluation. The problem facing contemporary art is that it has renounced the concept of beautiful as Kant defined it, as a judgement not determined by any concept and therefore universalisable. This art also confronts the crisis of criteria previously mentioned, which is an aesthetic question linked to perception, or in other words the materialisation and actual occurrence of an object that is not me, since we can only perceive the material. Today we have to think about and define the elements of the ecology of the material milieu of the mind artists are making use of in the current context, i.e. the hyperindustrial sphere. If the art world doesn't advance in developing an intelligent understanding of the questions, we'll pay a heavy price. The question of criteria will not resolve itself spontaneously; it's up to us to differentiate. We have to invent differences. And art cannot avoid critical work in the Kantian sense, a questioning of the relationship between technics, art, industry and the *We*.

In this sense, I feel that the Institut de recherche et coordination acoustique/musique (IRCAM) is a good place for working to reverse the terrible cultural entropy all around us. Music is the starting point for the concepts I've sketched out here. The concept of the musical instrument is the best starting point for thinking about technology. Music was and is the first manifestation of the culture industry: we hear music absolutely everywhere, not just on the radio and in discotheques and on home sound systems, and sometimes in concert, but also in airports, lifts, at the hairdresser's and in cars. Today, when temporal objects occupy such an enormous place in our lives, it is an extraordinary opportunity to be at the IRCAM, which is a space for the culture of invention, independent of industry, a simultaneously artistic and technological centre for the formalisation of temporal objects and organs of temporalisation.

Notes

This interview was previously published in *Artpress*, 276 (2001), pp. 15–19 (translation by L.-S. Torgoff).

1. Immanuel Kant, 'What Does It Mean to Orient Oneself in Thinking? (1786)', in *Religion and Rational Theology*, ed. and trans. Allen W. Wood and George di Giovanni (Cambridge: Cambridge University Press, 2008), pp. 1–18.
2. Jorge Luis Borges, 'Funes, His Memory', in *Fictions*, trans. Maria Kodama (London: Penguin, 2000), pp. 91–9.
3. Jeremy Rifkin, *The Age of Access: How the Shift from Ownership to Access is Transforming Modern Life* (London: Penguin, 2001).

Appendix 2. Becoming the Quasi-Cause of the Accident: Interview with Benoît Dillet

23 December 2014, Institute for Research and Innovation (IRI), Centre Georges Pompidou, Paris

Benoît Dillet (BD): In your Philosophising by Accident, *you present your relation to technics and technology as well as the extent to which your philosophical approach is influenced by your reading of Plato. These interviews provide an overall assessment of your trajectory over the course of the first three volumes of the* Technics and Time *series as well as opening up new inquiries that you developed in other works after 2004. I would like to test the hypothetical periodisation that I formulated as a reader of your work. I found three periods in your work: first the three volumes of* Technics and Time *(1994–2001); then three more series between 2004 and 2006,* Disbelief and Discredit *(three volumes),* Symbolic Misery *(two volumes) and* Constituting Europe *(two volumes), which pose questions on political economy, aesthetics and European cultural politics respectively. A third period began in 2008, after the great recession, with books that turned to a positive pharmacology, such as* Taking Care *(2008),* For a New Critique of Political Economy *(2009),* What Makes Life Worth Living *(2010),* States of Shock *(2012) and* Pharmacology of the National Front *(2013). Ten years after the publication of these interviews with Élie During, could you explain what motivated these different projects and series? How do you understand retrospectively the logic that articulated these three phases that I briefly outlined?*

Bernard Stiegler (BS): The first two volumes of *Technics and Time* were taken from my doctoral dissertation, that I defended in 1992. The third volume was not at all part of my dissertation. I wrote it after working in the domain of archives and images at the Institut national de l'audiovisuel (INA) for three years. My introduction to the field of images functioned as a kind of necessary disinhibition before confronting Kant's *Critique of Pure Reason* and the question of schematism. At the heart of this third

volume was a rethinking of technics in light of the question of schematism. As an aside, Pietro Montani argues the same thing today, and this
is crucial since he is a specialist of Kant.[1] I have been announcing three
more volumes for a very long time now; they have yet to be published
and people often ask me why I do not write these next three volumes
rather than doing all of this – and it is a real question. The incident that
suspended the writing process of *Technics and Time* was the maturing of
the question of political economy. It created a state of emergency in my
work and I realised that it was no longer possible to do what I believe in
many respects to be indispensable: to go into the works of Husserl, Plato,
Heidegger or even Derrida. It is something that continues to be relevant,
and I feel a sense of incompleteness about this foundational work.

At the same time, there are emergencies. The first was 'To Love,
To Love Me, To Love Us', which was published before *Philosophising by
Accident*.[2] Following the initiative of Élie During and his interest in the
third volume of *Technics and Time*, the interviews included in *Philosophising
by Accident* were organised to develop the arguments from this third
volume. Then came a series of invitations, especially two at Cerisy-
la-Salle, including one on the constitutive condition of the *We*.[3] But
this conference presentation arrived after two fundamental events that
opened the twenty-first century: the September 11 attacks and the elec-
tion of Jean-Marie Le Pen for the second round of the French presidential elections. It was in this context that I reconsidered other priorities
and developed a critical agenda.

BD: However, when we read Symbolic Misery, *we find in-depth readings of
authors working in the aesthetic field, such as Paul Klee, Joseph Beuys, Andy Warhol
and Marcel Duchamp. It is therefore a new field of inquiry for your work that we
already encounter in an emerging state in* Philosophising by Accident. *I'm thinking for instance of your discussion of synchronisation and diachronisation introduced
in* Disbelief and Discredit, *although the two volumes of* Constituting Europe
*are perhaps more direct interventions with practical responses to panic-stricken politics
[*panique politique*]. These are not simply political manifestos or polemics, rather
they require a real engagement with the subject. They are long readings of precise
moments in the history of philosophy but also an encounter with new fields of inquiry
for you, such as aesthetics, for instance – they are not pamphlets.*

BS: Ah no, they are not pamphlets, far from it, and I hate pamphlets!
When I write a book, I try to treat questions philosophically, at least for

now; it might change one day. Such is the dignity of thinking, even after my priorities changed. For a very long time now, I have wanted to write a fundamental work on Husserl's first philosophy, which is a very important text and not discussed enough, but given what is happening in the world, I have better things to do. This does not mean that I will not do this work, but if I end up writing it, it will be in reference to what is happening. In the last ten years, I have tried to maintain [*assurer*] philosophically the state of emergency. We are in a state of emergency on different levels: in relation to children – they are in a situation of desymbolisation that is extremely serious and irreversible; a state of emergency at the political level, with the far right dominating everywhere – maybe there are exceptions but I do not see them . . .

BD: . . . maybe in Spain . . .

BS: . . . Yes, Spain is currently left relatively untouched by the far right, but this comes after thirty-five years of Francoism! And there are other emergencies like the question of the Anthropocene that I introduced in my lecture at the General Organology conference at the University of Kent in Canterbury (UK). Today I write in this context. I have to share something: one day I was having dinner with Jacques Derrida at his place, at the end of the 1990s or perhaps in 2000. He had come back from South Africa, where he went regularly since he wrote on apartheid and Mandela. He tells me: 'It's incredible that people there study Heidegger and Husserl while their country is doing so badly. How can they do this?' I replied to him that in our country as well, things are also going very badly. What I am trying to get at is that, from the beginning, philosophy was born in a state of emergency. Socrates explains this very clearly: when he starts philosophising, it is in front of the Thirty Tyrants (who ruled Athens after the defeat in the Peloponnesian War in 404 BCE), in face of civil war. Philosophy does not happen in peace [*quiétude*]; this is what Hegel theorised.

Now, to answer the question: how do we keep philosophical rigour when we want to confront these things? *Symbolic Misery* is a very theoretical text – there are analyses of Freud, Darwin, Beuys and so on – but it starts with a text that was displayed in all the theatres in France, when those workers known as the *intermittents du spectacle* were on strike and prohibited the organisation of the Avignon festival.[4] As the director of the Institut de recherche et coordination acoustique/musique

(IRCAM), I was invited by France Culture and Laure Adler (who was France Culture's director at that time) to Cabaret Sauvage for a discussion with the *intermittents du spectacle*. This discussion was the origin of *Symbolic Misery*. All these texts were always anchored in the events of the twenty-first century – these are texts from the early twenty-first century. Moving on to what I am trying to do in these texts: others have reproached me for analysing short news items [*faits divers*], especially in the case of Richard Durn.[5] But for me these are not at all 'trivial news' but tragedies. It becomes trivial news with the media, and I tried to deconstruct this in order to turn this news story into philosophical questions. It is true that these events dominated my work in this period, up until *Constituting Europe*.[6] There is a second period in my work that begins with the fall of the Twin Towers and that ends with the two volumes *Constituting Europe*, which had a political objective: to participate in the debate on the European constitution.[7]

BD: This also coincided with the creation of your association Ars Industrialis . . .

BS: Exactly, Ars Industrialis was born in all this. My working methods changed with Ars Industrialis; they became much more collaborative. For instance, *The Re-Enchantment of the World* is a collective text, and, more generally, all my books at that time drew from a collective work.[8] Ars Industrialis really functioned as a group, and it continues to work this way, even though the registers have evolved over time. Ars Industrialis works differently now compared to earlier. One aspect of this transformation is the funding; it receives much less public funding than it used to, but it continues to enjoy a lot of support. New concepts were produced there: circuits of transindividuation, contributive economy, techniques of the self, and many other things.[9] Fundamental concepts, such as general organology which came before Ars Industrialis, were linked not only to the news related to the *intermittents du spectacle*, but also to my work in IRCAM.

In fact, my work at INA (between 1996 and 1999) led me to the question of schematism in Kant when I observed the work of the image in the industry of images at the end of the twentieth century. Then, I observed the question of time and artificial supports at IRCAM in organology, but at that time only in relation to music, as an organologist who studies music instruments. With the creation of Ars Industrialis, things changed at the level of the working environment and methods, and André Gorz's work had increasingly entered my thought, particularly influencing my conception of a contributive economy. This became a collective work, with around a dozen core members – this can be witnessed in the references in my texts during this period. There is also the co-written book with Christian Fauré and Alain Giffard,[10] but all these works drew upon the contributions of the members of the governing board of Ars Industrialis, like Frank Cormerais and Arnaud de Lepine and others. There are now so many people involved, particularly in the philosophical school and the website <pharmakon.fr>.

BD: There are two main themes that I want to address with you: first, your understanding of accidentality that forms the central, and underdeveloped, theme in the interviews included in Philosophising by Accident, *and the second theme is your philosophical work before 1994 and the publication of* Technics and Time 1. *The theme of accidentality is present throughout the interviews with Élie During, but can you explain how you approach the difference between accidentality and the event? I am thinking in particular of a passage from Deleuze's* The Logic of Sense *contrasting these two concepts:*

Events are ideal. Novalis says that there are two courses of events, one of them ideal, the other real and imperfect – for example, ideal Protestantism and real Lutheranism. The distinction however is not between two sorts of events; rather, it is between the event, which is ideal in nature, and its spatio-temporal realization in a state of affairs. The distinction is between event *and* accident.[11]

In The Logic of Sense, *quasi-causality transforms what happens, the accident, into an event. To put it differently, accident is what happens to existence while the event is a composition of singularities which is in 'the unlimited* Aion, *the Infinitive in which they subsist and insist'.*

BS: This book by Deleuze is the first of his books that I read, I think, a long time ago, around 1979. Like many books by Deleuze, I have left it in a dormant state for a long time, since it was extremely difficult to work on phenomenology, Heidegger, Husserl, Derrida together with Deleuze. This was a choice. The relations between the Derridians and the Deleuzians were extremely tense at that time, but not between Derrida and Deleuze. One should not confuse Deleuze with the Deleuzians. For instance, for Deleuzians, to work on Husserl did not make any sense, even though this is nonsense since Husserl and much of phenomenology were very important to Deleuze. Heidegger was one of his first interlocutors, contrary to what many young, naive Deleuzians believe. At some point, one needs to make some choices and it is very difficult to navigate in both Bergson and Husserl, and at the same time in Deleuze and Derrida – it is almost impossible, actually. I read Deleuze's texts at that time, and I also relied on Joël Bosquet, particularly for very personal reasons. I used Bosquet's words to survive but without really theorising them. Now I theorise them, and quasi-causality has almost become my weapon, Deleuze's weapon that he took elsewhere; Nietzsche would have said the spear. I tried to document this question with Simondon, with a part of Simondon's work that was not known to Deleuze.

Coming to your question about the event: for Deleuze, the event is what happens [*ce qui arrive*] in general, and what produces what happens to me. And 'to become what happens to me' is closely related to the transindividual and transindividuation.[12] This point is not really central to Deleuze, since he never uses Simondon's notion of the transindividual but borrows the concept of pre-individual instead. The neo-Deleuzians rush and make big mistakes, particularly when they see in the transindividual the unification of singularities, which cannot be further from Simondon's conception of the transindividual. This question of the event – which refers back to the accident for me, and thus to the originary default of origin, that is, the Accident – is what structures absolutely my entire thinking on technics. When I develop the question of the 'double *epokhal* redoubling', in truth what is at stake is the event that goes through a fundamental facticity (and on this point Deleuze would no longer agree with me), since any given accident is artificial [*factice*], it is in the very nature of the accident – outside of causal series, there is no essence. The event is accidental but not essential, except when quasi-causality will make this accidentality a necessity, not an essence but a necessity, and it will be inscribed in a quasi-causal series where there are no series. But as for me, I always bring this back to what Canguilhem called 'technical life'. It is this technical life in its entirety that matters. And today, we live an absolutely stunning acceleration of technological shocks, in need of being transformed into a necessity. This is what I call therapeutics of the *pharmakon*, which is completely homogeneous with Deleuze, even though I do not think Deleuze would have put it this way – but perhaps Félix Guattari would have.

BD: For Deleuze, the event-Idea comes after the accident, in contrast to Plato in Meno, *who argues that we only recognise what we already knew; this is* anamnesis *or reminiscence. This is the text that you discuss in* Philosophising by Accident, *but it is also a core moment of the first volume of* Technics and Time. *However, for you,* anamnesis *is always already conditioned by* hypomnesis, *as the artificial medium. Therefore, the event-Idea is for you technics, the arrival of technics and the invention to compose with accidentality. I would like to come back to the very heart of* Philosophising by Accident*: what is the relation between accidentality and technics, or hypomnesis? My second question follows from the first one: what is the relation between accidentality and intermittence in your work more broadly? It seems important to me to link these questions, since the theme of intermittence takes an increasingly central place in your work after 2003, after those radio interviews.*

BS: All forms of life, and not only noetic life, confront accidents. Technical life is not simply confronted by accidents, but it is constituted by accidentality. It is natively accidental and this is why the myth of Prometheus and Epimetheus shows a birth by accident. It is by accident (Epimetheus' forgetfulness) that life arrives if we revisit this myth. It is by accident that new living species – noetic species – need to be created. If we refer to a more scientific or anthropological register – and my theories are only theories – we do not know for sure, and to my mind we will never know, since this is precisely the originary default of origin. We will never be able to find this origin since by nature this origin lacks [*fait défaut*]; we will always need to theorise it. Today, it is perhaps a somewhat dated theory, but the notorious question of the Rift Valley in Kenya, which explains the conquest of mobility, is an accident. It is close to Rousseau's ecliptic – in his case it is a divine accident, but nonetheless it is an accident. In general, when we try to theorise on the origin of the human, we stumble across an accident every time. The original sin is an accident. In Taoism, there is also a myth very close to the myth of Prometheus and Epimetheus, and so on. All this always produces artifice, that is, what will fill in [*combler*] artificially the accident of the lack, what I call the default.

*BD: But is it not more a matter of composing rather than making up or filling in [*combler*]?*

BS: Indeed, it is never fully filled in since, as Freud shows, as soon as it is filled in, an even greater gap [*comble*] is created, according to the logic of the *pharmakon*. This is done through the process of externalisation. The more the accident is *compensated*, the more it grows, and the greater the compensation needs to be, and this is endless. It is the myth of Sisyphus.

Now, concerning intermittence, we need to come back to the question of quasi-causality and the event from earlier, but also that of the double *epokhal* redoubling – which, to put it very plainly, posits that the technical accident starts a system-making process with other accidents, eventually developing an entire technical system. The system has its own internal logic, what I call technical individuation. This is what makes this system seem autonomous at times, but in reality it is not autonomous. It is true that it secretes its own developing logic, and that it constantly misadjusts itself. This is lived as an accident or what I called a 'technological shock'.[13] Disorientating and stupefying epochs are produced, where circuits of transindividuation as a whole are disturbed. Then comes a second period, where circuits recompose themselves, and there existences reappear since in the first period we are in *subsistence* – a situation when one is only concerned with survival and self-preservation.[14] *Existences* reappear when characters [*personnages*] are produced, they invent something new. At the end of this process, something comes together: *consistence*. A new age of consistence is constituted but it immediately starts to disappear. This is crucial, and in a way it corresponds to the theory of phases of being in Simondon – nothing is given once and for all. These are the event-Ideas that you mentioned earlier: at some point, something that is more than existing is produced. This is what consists and creates what Deleuze calls the 'plane of consistency', even though it is not so clearly expressed in Deleuze (and Guattari) and there are other ways to interpret it. I do not think the way I interpret it is in complete contradiction with Deleuze.

BD: But is intermittence essential? We know that it takes place among subsistence, existence and consistence, but in your work, the question of intermittence comes at times on extremely practical registers such as the question of work, when you dialogue with André Gorz and Maurizio Lazzarato, but at others, when you read Aristotle's On the Soul, *it becomes – and I know you don't like this word – ontology.[15]*

BS: No, it is not an ontology . . .

BD: . . . What about an ontogenesis?

BS: It proceeds from an Aristotelian ontology. In fact, I think this from Freud; it is linked to desire and therefore to Spinoza and Hegel, who are both great thinkers of desire. I have an economy of subsistence, existence and consistence that is quite clear and invariable. I am really at peace with this. I argue – in a classical way – that existence is what no longer needs subsistence. Someone who exists is someone who does not ask himself where he is going to sleep tonight or what he is going to eat tonight; he has time ahead of himself. Thus he has time to devote to his narcissism – I do not use the word 'narcissism' in a pejorative sense but rather in the sense of 'auto-affection'. We do not exist without auto-affection, which is narcissistic (according to Freud), and this is what Hegel calls 'self-consciousness', if we refer to the history of philosophy. But I argue that an existence exists when it is capable of moving to consistence. I can only conquer a dimension other than subsistence when I am *capable* of going into the sphere of consistence: such is intermittency according to Aristotle. Sometimes I am capable of reaching this sphere and I know it, but most of the time I know it but I cannot arrive there, and other times I cannot reach it at all, but I know that others do – such is noetic life. You referred to ontology, and in fact the thought of intermittence starts from Platonic ontology interpreted by Aristotle, but for me it is a return to the tragic. The great thinkers of intermittency were tragic thinkers. The tragic condition can be expressed this way: I cannot reach truth qua truth. Truth is always fugitive or transient, accidental, quasi-causal, and it always needs to be reconstructed, in contrast to Zeus' self-presence.

BD: Intermittency in France is almost synonymous with precarity, and yet it is a positive concept for you. Intermittent work is defined by periods of intense work in employment with periods of unemployment, which are considered 'work time outside unemployment', as you put it with Gorz.[16] It is also a work scheme for those working in the cultural sector: they are called intermittents du spectacle. *How do you reconcile questions of intermittency in Aristotle, Spinoza and Hegel, and these practical questions linked to the status of the* intermittent du spectacle, *whose dossier is currently sitting on the Minister of Culture Fleur Pellerin's desk, waiting for a new reform? Should this working condition be understood more broadly and encompass creative and freelance employments in the contributive or sharing economy?*

BS: This is one of the themes of my last book, *The Automatic Society*, which ends on these questions, but with Ars Industrialis, we have been thinking about these questions for a long time.[17] For me this regime of exception (the *intermittents du spectacle*) should become the rule since employment will disappear. I do not think employment should be replaced by precarity, but by a contributive income that does away with precarity. Precarity is a condition that leaves oneself in subsistence. At the time of writing the *Disbelief and Discredit* series, I planned a fourth volume entitled *The Aristocracy to Come*, and my goal is to constitute this aristocracy, so that everyone can become an aristocrat, and therefore live outside subsistence. Aristocrats do not need to think about subsisting. They are ready to die, but in Ancient Greece this meant to be ready to fight against Sparta and to remain in the field of honour. To be ready to die today means to be ready to change, to accept the accident and to become its quasi-cause. Today, this is not a utopia but the only rational way to face the fast economic development of robots that, as many studies show, will destroy employment and will lead to problems in terms of solvency, purchasing power and so on. We should therefore introduce redistribution on other criteria. A rational perspective on the economic context today works at making sure that in fifty years, the temperature of the Earth has not risen, that we are not resorting to cannibalism or mass killings to support nine billion people. We need negentropy produced by intermittency.

BD: I would like to come back to the important steps towards the writing of Technics and Time. *Your readings and borrowings of Leroi-Gourhan's theories were particularly important to your arguments in the first volume of* Technics and Time. *Those theories counted even more than Simondon, whom you read much later. Can you explain how you encountered Leroi-Gourhan's work?*

BS: I encountered Leroi-Gourhan in Derrida's *Of Grammatology*. I was a student at that time, and I bought all the books that Derrida referred to in *Of Grammatology*: Saussure, Lévi-Strauss, Leibniz, Heidegger, Rousseau and others. I wanted to appropriate this book as much as possible. It is an important book to me: it was a dazzling sight, a vision, something happened and I tried to cultivate all of this more than Derrida himself, since Derrida gave up at some point. This is why I am very proud that Sylvain Auroux will soon be translated into English.[18] After reading Leroi-Gourhan, I tried archaeology and prehistory. When I got out of prison, I went to his laboratory; he was no longer there but his team remained at Meudon, directed by François Audouze. I met and worked with a lot of prehistorians. I wrote articles for *Les Nouvelles de l'archéologie*.[19] I gave a seminar at the Collège international de philosophie for a few years, and one of the researchers from Leroi-Gourhan's team, Jean-

Paul Demoule, participated in my seminar. I worked a lot with archaeologists, and when I refer to tertiary retentions, I do not only refer to
computers but also flints – I had the chance to dig. My encounter with
Simondon took place later, around 1986, on François Laruelle's advice,
but as for Leroi-Gourhan, I read him from 1979.

*BD: Can you explain how crucial is Leroi-Gourhan's thought to the question of origin,
discussed in the first volume of* Technics and Time, *and particularly how material
traces require a more material approach? Plato remains at the level of ideas in* Meno,
while with Leroi-Gourhan, you seek materials . . .

BS: I am a spiritualist materialist, since I do not at all oppose spirit and
matter. I think that there is a hypermatter that is more than matter, and
on this point I refer to quantum physics, but in different terms.[20] What
interested me so deeply in archaeology were the traces, and here I am
extremely critical of Derrida and his concept of 'arche-trace'. It is an
empty concept: there are traces but 'arche-trace' cannot exist, and traces
are always accidental. To him, arche-trace is the essence of the trace, but
there can be no essence to the trace. What makes a trace is precisely the
absence of essence. There is nothing but traces: they are hard, like relics,
they are what has vanished [*de l'évanoui*], and they are also promises, like
protentions, and thus inexistence and consistence. It is extremely moving
to find a flint. Once I found one by chance, by accident, while planting
a tree. I have a really practical, empirical and experiential relation to the
concept of tertiary retention. I try to create concepts that are at times
very abstract and formalised, but at the same time I try not to lose sight
of their relation to the material and empirical trace. This is why my relation to Leroi-Gourhan is essential. On the other hand, I have a problem
with Simondon, and this is part of a larger debate I have with Yuk Hui
and Jean-Hugues Barthélémy, who are more Simondonian than I am.[21]
I have never agreed with Simondon's concept of information: he argues
that we can dissociate information from matter. I do not believe this is
possible. A unit of information always carries with it its medium and its
conditions. We cannot see this but that does not mean it does not exist.
This is what organology is all about, to claim that traces are always
conditioned by their organs of production.

*BD: To continue with your intellectual and practical journey in the 1980s up until
1994 with the publication of* Technics and Time: *how did this period affect your*

understanding of the difficult relations between theory and practice? I am thinking, for instance, of the propositions you made to the government in the 1980s. They seem to prepare for the arguments of Technics and Time, *before your involvement at INA and its influence on your redefinition of schematism, after Kant.*

BS: In 1984, I was a member of the Collège international de philosophie. The engineer Thierry Gaudin participated in my seminar and brought in his entire team. At the end of these seminars, he suggested investing in a project on digital technologies if I could find other sources of funding. I let Derrida know that I wanted to make some propositions to the Ministry of Culture to work on digital technologies. I was working on this since my topic at that time was Plato's conception of *hypomnesis*. This was when floppy disks, Minitels and telematics were around. I found myself *chargé de mission* for the French government, and with a salary. The title of the study was 'The Philosophical Challenges of New Information Technologies'. I worked on this study for one year, and I delivered the report at the Château de Vincennes to a jury composed of Derrida, Michel Deguy, Jean-François Lyotard, Jean-Luc Godard and Pierre-Jean Labarrière. Based on this report, the Centre Georges Pompidou decided to organise an exhibition. During two years, between 1985 and 1987, I worked on this exhibition called *Memories of the Future*, and I developed relationships with INA personnel. One year before *Memories of the Future*, Lyotard also proposed his exhibition *The Immaterials*. I participated in the creation of the electronic system *épreuves d'écriture* (writing tests) since I was very close to Lyotard at that time.[22]

After *Memories of the Future*, I learned that Jacques Attali (President Mitterrand's advisor at that time) commissioned Michel Melot, who was the conservator of the Georges Pompidou Centre's library and thus my line manager, as an external curator – I was working with a conservator as my line manager. Melot was commissioned by Attali to conceive a library based on my ideas from the exhibition: the famous 'Très Grande Bibliothèque' (TGB). Melot asked me to contribute to the Melot-Cahart report on electronic texts, and I wrote a section on 'reading stations' [*postes de lecture*].[23] At that time, I got a position at the Technological University of Compiègne, and in 1988 I submitted to the Ministry of Research a report on computer-aided reading and writing. It called for the development of a literary software on CD-ROM, but the Ministry replied that this project would only be supported if the TGB project integrated the project of reading stations. This is how I started my employment at the Bibliothèque nationale de France, which was then called Établissement public pour la bibliothèque de France.

For almost three years I was directing a research group ('Département nouvelles technologies'), composed of fifteen people including someone from INA, to develop machines called 'Postes de Lectures Assistées par Ordinateurs' (PLAO) (computer-aided reading stations).[24] While the internet did not exist, we had the idea to develop GML language – which is a hypertext language – to create exchange formats for the first modems and systems of communication by phone to exchange files, but also to think of annotating languages to share corpuses and to read collectively the corpuses and so on. In 1993 came a new government and the new Prime Minister Édouard Balladur ended these projects, both for our team and for my own job. In 1993, I am laid off and everything is stopped. One should not forget that for the Bibliothèque nationale de France this was first and foremost a project of a server-centre to digitise seven million books.[25] If this had been done, it would have been the world's first data centre! It is partly Mitterrand's fault, since he wanted an imposing building, and all the money went into the architecture. This was a catastrophe, since France was at the forefront of digital innovation at that time.

BD: In the interviews contained in Philosophising by Accident, *you introduce some elements that would make up the next volumes of* Technics and Time. *Discussions and analyses of Plato, Freud, the notion of idiotext and the 'necessary default'* [le défaut qu'il faut], *the atranscendental as default of origin, and so on. As a reader, I wonder: what place did these future projects occupy in your work?*

BS: I've always thought that the last part of my doctoral dissertation, called 'The Idiot', and in which the concept of idiotext is central, is not publishable. I have not published it yet since I do not think it is ready. The first presentation was there in my dissertation, but a dissertation is not a book. Jean-Luc Marion thought that it was the most interesting part of it all, and he wanted to publish it with Presses Universitaires de France.[26] I did not want to publish it so soon. If I did not continue the *Technics and Time* series, it is not only due to the fall of the Twin Towers in September 2001, but also to the insufficient maturation of this work. The last part of my dissertation on idiotext, on spirals and other things, is not far from Leibniz and Whitehead; it is very speculative. Behind these speculations are great ambitions. It is not about ontology or the transcendental; indeed, I try precisely to leave those realms, referring to the atranscendental. I tried in this last part to establish what long ago we would have called 'Principles for an Atranscendental Philosophy'. To me, this is what philosophy is about. In other words, I have not yet started the labour of philosophy, and perhaps I will never devote myself to this – maybe I will not have time. It is true that, at times in my recent books, I have introduced briefly some of these ideas. I try, on the other hand, to gather the conditions to make all this express-ible, but for the moment it is not possible. If it comes to light, it will be a long dialogue with Bergson, Jacques Lacan and questions raised by Heidegger in *Being and Time*, among other things. Two volumes of *Technics and Time* remain to be written: *Symbols and Diabols*, on Plato and philosophy in Ancient Greece, and *The War of Spirits*, which discusses at length Sylvain Auroux's work that I only discovered in 1993. These two volumes were not part of my dissertation, but there are traces of these materials in it and in my lectures on ancient philosophy at the University of Compiègne.

Notes

1. Pietro Montani, *Bioestetica: Senso comune, tecnica e arte nell'età della globaliz-zazione* (Rome: Carocci, 2007), and *Tecnologie della sensibilità: Estetica e immaginazione interattiva* (Milan: Cortina Raffaello, 2014).
2. Bernard Stiegler, 'To Love, To Love Me, To Love Us: From September 11 to April 21', in *Acting Out*, trans. David Barison, Daniel Ross and Patrick Crogan (Stanford: Stanford University Press, 2008), pp. 37–82.
3. The lecture was originally entitled 'Of the I and the We: Working Together in the City' and published as 'To Love, To Love Me, To Love Us, Part I', in *Acting Out*, pp. 37–59.
4. *Intermittents du spectacle* are artists and technicians working in the cultural economy (theatre and cinema, mostly); their special status grants them benefits when they are out of work or in between two projects. These benefits are different from unemployment benefits, both financially and morally. See Pierre-Michel Menger, *Les intermittents du spectacle: Sociologie d'une exception* (Paris: Éditions EHESS, 2005), and Antonella Corsani and Maurizio Lazzarato, *Intermittents et Précaires* (Paris: Éditions Amsterdam, 2008).
5. Richard Durn murdered eight members of the Nanterre city council on 26 March 2002, and committed suicide two days later. For an analysis

of Durn's diaries and killings, see Stiegler, 'To Love, To Love Me, To Love Us, Part I'.

6. Bernard Stiegler, *Constituer l'Europe, 1: Dans un monde sans vergogne* (Paris: Galilée, 2005), and *Constituer l'Europe, 2: Le motif européen* (Paris: Galilée, 2005).

7. A referendum on the project of a European constitution was organised in France on 29 May 2005, in which a majority of voters rejected the project (54.68% of the voters). The European constitution was, however, passed a few years later by the Parliament.

8. Bernard Stiegler and Ars Industrialis, *The Re-Enchantment of the World: The Value of Spirit against Industrial Populism*, trans. Trevor Arthur (London: Bloomsbury, 2014).

9. Definitions and contextualisations of these concepts can be found in Victor Petit, 'Vocabulaire d'Ars Industrialis', in Bernard Stiegler, *Pharmacologie du Front national* (Paris: Flammarion, 2013), pp. 369–441.

10. Bernard Stiegler, Alain Giffard and Christian Fauré, *Pour en finir avec la mécroissance: Quelques réflexions d'Ars Industrialis* (Paris: Flammarion, 2009).

11. Gilles Deleuze, *The Logic of Sense*, trans. Mark Lester with Charles Stivale (London: The Athlone Press, 1990), p. 53.

12. 'To become the offspring of one's events and not of one's actions, for the action is itself produced by the offspring of the event.' Deleuze, *The Logic of Sense*, p. 150. See also Stiegler, *Pharmacologie du Front national*, pp. 288–91.

13. See Bernard Stiegler, *States of Shock: Stupidity and Knowledge in the Twenty-First Century*, trans. Daniel Ross (Cambridge: Polity Press, 2015).

14. For distinctions between existence, consistence and subsistence, to which political insistence needs to be added, see Bernard Stiegler, *Disbelief and Discredit, Vol. 1: The Decadence of Industrial Democracies*, trans. Daniel Ross and Suzanne Arnold (Cambridge: Polity Press, 2011).

15. Aristotle, *De Anima: On the Soul*, trans. Hugh Lawson-Tancred (London: Penguin, 1986); Stiegler, *Disbelief and Discredit, Vol. 1*, pp. 131–62.

16. Bernard Stiegler, *For a New Critique of Political Economy*, trans. Daniel Ross (Cambridge: Polity Press, 2010), p. 22.

17. Bernard Stiegler, *La Société automatique, Vol. 1: L'Avenir du travail* (Paris: Fayard, 2015).

18. Sylvain Auroux, *La Révolution technologique de la grammatisation* (Liège: Mardaga, 1994).

19. Bernard Stiegler, 'Leroi-Gourhan, part maudite de l'anthropologie', *Les Nouvelles de l'archéologie*, 48–9 (1992), pp. 23–30, and 'La

120   Philosophising by Accident

Programmatologie de Leroi-Gourhan', *Les Nouvelles de l'archéologie*, 48–9 (1992), pp. 31–6.

20. Bernard Stiegler, *Économie de l'hypermatériel et psychopouvoir: Entretiens avec Philippe Petit et Vincent Bontems* (Paris: Mille et une nuits, 2008).

21. Yuk Hui, *On the Existence of Digital Objects* (Minneapolis: University of Minnesota Press, 2016); Jean-Hugues Barthélémy, 'De Simondon à Stiegler via Leroi-Gourhan: La Refondation artefactuelle du "transindividuel"', in Benoît Dillet and Alain Jugnon (eds), *Technologiques: La Pharmacie de Bernard Stiegler* (Nantes: Cécile Defaut, 2013), pp. 247–64.

22. Yuk Hui and Andreas Broeckmann (eds), *30 Years after* Les Immatériaux: *Art, Science, and Theory* (Berlin: Meson Press, 2015).

23. Patrice Cahart and Michel Melot, *Propositions pour une grande bibliothèque. Rapport au Premier ministre* (Paris: La Documentation française, 1989).

24. Daniel Renoult and Jacqueline Melet-Sanson (eds), *La Bibliothèque nationale de France: Collections, services, publics* (Paris: Éditions du Cercle de la Librairie, 2001); Jean-Marc Mandosio, *L'Effondrement de la très grande bibliothèque nationale de France, ses causes, ses conséquences* (Paris: Éditions de l'Encyclopédie des Nuisances, 1999).

25. For a comparison of three different models of digitisation at the Bibliothèque nationale de France, the British Library and the Österreichische Nationalbibliothek, see Gaëlle Béquet, *Trois bibliothèques européennes face à Google: Aux origines de la bibliothèque numérique (1990–2010)* (Paris: Publications de l'École des Chartes, 2015).

26. Jean-Luc Marion is the current editor of the famous and important philosophy book series *Épiméthée* at Presses Universitaires de France.

Index